Time Management

Be More Productive and Build Habits of Most Successful People

(Understand the Universal Rules of Life and Organize Your Day With These Easy to Use Time Management Hacks)

Floyd Wallace

© Copyright 2022

Published By **Bella Frost**

Floyd Wallace

All Rights Reserved

Time Management: Be More Productive and Build Habits of Most Successful People (Understand the Universal Rules of Life and Organize Your Day With These Easy to Use Time Management Hacks)

ISBN 978-1-77485-463-1

All rights reserved. No part of this guidebook shall be reproduced in any form without permission in writing from the publisher except in the case of brief quotations embodied in critical articles or reviews.

Legal & Disclaimer

The information contained in this ebook is not designed to replace or take the place of any form of medicine or professional medical advice. The information in this ebook has been provided for educational & entertainment purposes only.

The information contained in this book has been compiled from sources deemed reliable, and it is accurate to the best of the Author's knowledge; however, the Author cannot guarantee its accuracy and validity and cannot be held liable for any errors or omissions. Changes are periodically made to this book. You must consult your doctor or get professional medical advice before using any of the suggested remedies, techniques, or information in this book.

Upon using the information contained in this book, you agree to hold harmless the Author from and against any damages, costs, and expenses, including any legal fees potentially resulting from the application of any of the information provided by this guide. This disclaimer applies to any damages or injury caused by the use and application, whether directly or indirectly, of any advice or information presented, whether for breach of contract, tort, negligence, personal injury, criminal intent, or under any other cause of action.

You agree to accept all risks of using the information presented inside this book. You need to consult a professional medical practitioner in order to ensure you are both able and healthy enough to participate in this program.

Table of Contents

Chapter 1: Why You Should Be Concerned About Time Management?.. 1

Chapter 2: What To Do To Plan Your Week................. 4

Chapter 3: Keep Track Of The Time You Spend On Different Tasks 18

CHAPTER 4: Goal Management.................................22

Chapter 5: Making Attitude Changes 38

Chapter 6: Tips To Better Manage Our Time Is Time To Control... 51

Chapter 7: Inhibiting Response For Children 60

Chapter 8: Deadlines For Meetings............................75

Chapter 9: Time Tools For Management 79

Chapter 10: How To Manage People In Your Life 87

Chapter 11: Managing Obstacles 95

Chapter 12: Improvement Of Your Focus In Your Work To Improve Your Productivity 109

Chapter 13: Steps To Take To Time Management ...115

CHAPTER 14: HOW TO BUILD And RETAIN Active Habits...133

Chapter 15: Applying Your 5 Year Vision 149

Chapter 16: Physical Side Of Time Management.....161

Chapter 17: What To Do To Prevent Overextending Yourself 171

Chapter 18: Importance To Self-Care For Time Management 176

Chapter 1: Why You Should Be Concerned About Time Management?

We are constantly talking about managing time, but do you know what it actually means. The term "time management" generally refers to the way you plan and plan your day to accomplish the tasks that you've defined. Although it may be counterintuitive to devote your time to study about time management instead of taking advantage of your time to focus on the business you run, but in reality, you might be pleasantly surprised by the huge advantages that understanding time management brings. This includes lower stress levels, higher effectiveness and efficiency, an improved professional reputation, more chances to pursue important personal and professional goals as well as increased chances to advance. Additionally, the negative consequences of not being able to properly manage your time include missing deadlines, poor quality work and inefficient workflow as well as increased stress levels and a negative professional image. How often do you notice yourself wasting hours, days, every week? For the majority of people, there's never enough time to accomplish all of their work. Before you proceed, think about these questions things: Are the tasks that you take on in the course of the day most important? Are you often doing things at the end of the day, or wanting more time? Do you make sure you have time to plan and plan your tasks?

Do you know the amount of time you're putting into every task you complete? Do you often find yourself interrupted during your work? Do you establish goals to help you determine what things you must focus on? Do you have room for emergency tasks on your agenda to deal with the unexpected?

Are you aware of whether the projects you're doing are of low, medium or high-value? If you are given a new project Do you evaluate the importance of it and prioritize it accordingly? Are you overwhelmed by deadlines and commitments? Are distractions preventing your ability to complete crucial projects?

Do you frequently find yourself doing work from home to finish it? Do you typically discuss that you are on the right track with boss? But when you decide to do the task you want to do is it a good idea to take the time to evaluate whether the outcomes are worth the effort spent?

If you're having trouble answering these questions, you may need to tackle the task of managing your time. In the following sections, we'll take look at a couple of tools to assist you manage your time effectively.

Chapter 2: What To Do To Plan Your Week

A week-long calendar is among the most efficient time management tools , and it is essential for your success. The calendar will enable you to navigate the week and provide you with an overview of all the tasks you must accomplish every day. If you take a little step every day, you'll be able to move one step towards achieving your personal goals. The seven actions that you should follow to organize your week effectively that are described in the following chapters.

Step 1: Get a Calendaring Tool

The first step towards success is to purchase an application for calendaring. There are a few popular alternatives, which are the pen and paper and the option of an online calendar. Both come with their advantages and drawbacks, but in the present, the majority of people use pen and paper.

The drawback of this method is that it's tiring as you have to record hundreds of things using a pen. Furthermore, if choose to change the order of your list of tasks You can erase things that you wrote with pencil, but the paper will remain filthy.

Additionally, you'll need keep a physical copy of your calendar, which will take up space. If you do lose your calendar, you won't be able to make a new plan. But this method does not require electricity, which is the reason why it is still used widely.

Another alternative is to get the option of having an online calendar. There are many different ways and applications/programs for keeping your calendar. If you don't want expensive programs and applications, you can have an Excel calendar. Microsoft Excel.

The benefit of having an online calendar is it's extremely simple to alter your calendar. It is simple to drag and down or paste various entries.

Additionally, you could use your calendar with your smartphone, which you will likely carry every day. This means you will not have to carry extra items to track your progress or things you'll need to accomplish throughout the week.

The downside to this technique is the fact that it needs electricity. For instance, if you're going on a camping trip or traveling with a small supply of electricity it could cause difficulties. If your computer is not powered by electricity then your calendar is inaccessible until you reach an electrical outlet.

Selecting a calendaring software is crucial, since you'll use it for a lot of months to come, so, it needs to be as relaxing for you as it can be.

Step 2: Locate an area that is free of distractions

When you're making plans, it's essential to focus, so the best location for this is a quiet space. You must eliminate all of the distractions and concentrate on your task you are working on. This is particularly important for people who have not thought about their week in advance since it is difficult to manage time in the beginning.

Third Step: Dumping Mind, and Activity Recall

In this chapter, I will discuss two concepts that comprise the Mind Dumping as well as Activity Recall. Both are essential to the effectiveness of your time-management and I'll start by describing them.

Mind Dumping
Mind Dumping is the process of dumping everything you have in your head onto an article of paper. In your situation, rather than writing your your thoughts, you should note down all the tasks you have to complete. The list of things to do is not required to be written in any specific arrangement, all you have to do is to make a list of everything you must do. If it's your life easier to note things down using keywords instead of writing a full descriptions of each goal insofar as you be aware of what each item relates to on the list.
The reason that mind dumping is essential to

your success is because it allows you clear your head. It allows you to arrange your thoughts in a much more efficient way and you will be able to recall more information. After you have completed the Mind Dump Activity, you must continue by completing Activity Recall.

Activity Recall
Activity Recall is the process of recollecting everything that occurred in the previous week. Through this exercise it can benefit you in two ways:

1. It can help you decide on the tasks you have to complete regularly for example. every month or each week
2. It allows you to reflect on the different ways you approach tasks.

If you know your routine activities, you'll be able determine your schedule in line with them. For instance, you could go to the gym on Wednesdays after work, so you can add to your weekly calendar "Go for a workout". If you're using an electronic calendars, a few calendars have the capability of defining a recurring occasion, which means that you can program it so to repeat each week and display your schedule of times accordingly.

I will also show the other benefit using an illustration. If you don't make an appointment at the local hairdresser because of an unplanned meeting at the office, it is important to think about the circumstances. In order to reduce the likelihood of this scenario occurring again, you can arrange your next appointment with your hairdresser later , and make sure you have time to attend unplanned meetings (especially when they occur frequently).

Step 4: Re-evaluate Your Life/Primary Goals and Divide them into smaller and Weekly Goals

Everyone has different goals for their lives. They might be buying an apartment or writing a novel flying, skydiving, or even traveling the globe. There are a myriad of objectives that people can set, and they can be attained if you be striving towards them. The most effective approach is to break your goal into smaller milestones and begin working toward each one.

The most effective way to reach your goals in life is to divide it into smaller pieces. For instance, if your have a goal to write a book you could note on your calendar to complete 1000 pages throughout the week. It could be that you'd like be able to compose 200-300 words from Monday to Friday and take the weekend and Sunday off to do other activities. That means you are sluggish, however, your goals are doable and achievable, just do instead of putting off. If you're feeling good during your week because you're able to achieve your goal, you could surpass your goals and write more than 1000 words.

If, on the other hand, you decide to complete the entire book over the course of a week which may not be achievable then you won't be content, since you won't be able to meet your objective. The result is that you are more productive, and also less enthusiastic.

Additionally, by dividing your goal into smaller pieces that you can solve different challenges that are related to the same goal simultaneously. When you look back on the process of writing your book, you might wish to spend the time to read what you've written a month ago to keep your mind sharp, and as a way to review your draft to make sure you have fixed errors by devoting one hour per day. This means that you're in a position to achieve the same endpoint of creating the book, but you're now doing the editing work instead of the writing part of your book is published.

To simplify the process to set your weekly goals, examine the list you made during the mind dump and recall exercises. Classify the various activities into the various objectives of your life.

Step 5: Prioritize, Diversify , and Take action

After you've recorded all of your objectives and categorized them then the next step is described in this chapter.

In the beginning, you must prioritize your goals This means you have to prioritize your goals and activities from the lowest priority to the most crucial. There are different priorities for different people and priorities, which are influenced by their requirements and preferences. For instance, reading the book is a major priority for a student because it provides the necessary information that will be required for the upcoming exam However, it might be an unimportant importance for a business person because there isn't enough time to sit down and read and instead there is a requirement to attend numerous business meetings.

Although the priority of the various activities or tasks will be different, you should prioritize them in at least three categories:

High Priority:
Determine which events are not movable and must be executed. Examples of these activities include events like weddings and birthdays, corporate gatherings and similar events.

Medium Priority:
The most important activities can be relocated, however you'd rather not move them. Some

examples of these activities might be a date, or a meeting with your buddies at the local bar. Write down any activities that require an huge amounts of time, like making plans for an excursion.

Low Priority:
Group activities are those that are easily relocated or canceled. Hobbies can also be included in this category.

After prioritizing your activity, you can make sure that your calendar is varied. This means that you'll be sure to making plans to keep your week interesting. If, for instance, you work at a work at a desk it could be interesting to explore new sports like the mountain climb or surf. The ocean waves or the mountains can give you a much-needed breaks.

If you are able to diversify your activities your options, you may also make room for unexpected events to take place. You might, for instance, get invited to a party at your house or to a party with close circle of friends. If you do not get invitations, you may take advantage of the time off to have an impulsive trip and take on activities that you didn't plan in the beginning like a short excursion to the beach, or a quick drive through your neighborhood.

After you've identified and varied the tasks you will be doing during your week Next step is to implement. This is where you write your tasks in a manner which you make use of action verbs. For instance, you could be writing to get ready for an upcoming presentation that you'll be presenting in the coming week, however in the action step you might create "Show your colleague my slides, and then practice together".

After you have completed the actionize it is now possible to visualize the action and are able to clearly define the actions you will follow. If you don't have clear guidelines or actions that you can follow, it is difficult to take action. For instance, if you go through "Presentation" it can be difficult to act according to your schedule. You aren't sure when you'll have to make the presentation, practice it, or watch someone other's presentation. This is why, when you follow this procedure, you'll be more motivated to accomplish what you'd like to accomplish.

Step 6: Create Your Calendar
When you begin writing down items on your calendar, be sure that you start with most important activities, and then begin with low priority activities, then lower priority tasks. This will make sure that you don't skip any important events and allocate a time slot for each of them.

If any of the top prioritised activities takes longer than you expected at the start You can shift your lower priority activity, or even cancel it depending on the type of activity.

It is also suggested to mark the prioritised activities with different shades. This helps you quickly see the variety of tasks you have to complete throughout the day without having to read the various tasks. I usually color high-priority activities with orange or red and medium priority with yellow, and low-priority by using green. But the color of your choice is your choice and based on the color you are able to associate with different prioritisations.

If you are unable to squeeze all the activities within your timetable then you should consider which activities are able to be cut or relocated. You can also examine your goals. If you are able to break it down into smaller chunks and make that happen and then write down the goals.

Step 7: Ensure You Follow Through To Your Plan

Once you've completed each step You should have a written list of the things you'd like to complete next week, colored them, moved and taken out some. The second step that is crucial which many people do not succeed at is sticking to the plan you've set. If something does not follow your schedule, you should not be afraid of changing things around. If you're not able to accomplish the majority of your planned actions, you may want to consider reducing activities or changing the goals.

Additionally, it could be tempting to reschedule all your planned activities and use the time to do other things like watching television. This is not the goal of making the plan and the subsequent chapters will discuss ways to remain active and motivated.

Chapter 3: Keep Track Of The Time You Spend On Different Tasks

You might think you're adept at estimating the time you are spending on different tasks. But, research has shown the fact that just 17% of the population can accurately calculate the time they put into their job. When we are working on a project that we are working on, we will spend more time doing it than we ought to. Even though we think we're doing something worthwhile however, the truth is that we're generally thinking about non-essential things, drawing or browsing the web. Katie 26, an elementary school teacher who is passionate about her job and is content with her work-life balance. But, two years ago, Katie wasn't as productive like she is today. She was a procrastinator with an unorganized lifestyle. A few days ago, she decided to make a change and started tracking the amount of time she would devote to her work. Once she started tracking the time she spent on various tasks, she realized that the majority times, she was showering, watching TV or organizing her clothes, choosing what outfit to wear next day for work, and checking her emails. Most of these tasks were not that significant and could easily be accomplished with less effort.

Katie was able to break down the tasks she performs every day in two groups: essential things and less important Then she began to track the time she spent on various tasks, and gradually cut the amount of time she spent on things that were not important. This assisted her in improving the routine of her life, as well as her productivity. If you're looking to be more productive in your life, you should start monitoring the time you devote doing various things.

How to track your time spent on activities

Here's how to apply this technique to boost your productivity and time management.

1. Examine your daily routine and create lists of all the various chores you participate in each day.

When you've made your list, look through your list of activities to evaluate their effects and significance in your daily life. For instance, if simply watch television, browse the web and chat with your friends on a daily basis Consider

what these activities can do for you and if they're effective in helping you to achieve something. If they aren't helping you in any way, then label these activities as insignificant.'
Take a look at the amount of time you put into each of the tasks you mentioned. Take a look at yourself for a couple of days and note down the times you do these tasks. This will help you understand how much time you're spending doing nothing or doing nothing at all.

If you are having trouble making it happen by yourself then you should consider using time-tracking tools like Rescue Time. This powerful tool will help to calculate how much time you are spending on regular tasks like typing, checking emails or using social media.

As you track your time, be aware of times when you feel most energetic and active during the daytime. This is when you are at your best and is also the most efficient time to tackle your essential chores. If you can complete your important tasks in this window of time helps increase your productivity.

Write down the amount of time you spend in various activities in order to determine if those activities actually help your life in some way. Review this list and you'll be amazed at how much time you spend each day and how much you are doing nothing but useless things. With an understanding of how you are using your time, you can move on to the next stage; become excited about being productive.

CHAPTER 4: Goal Management

The ability to set goals in a timely manner is essential to efficiently managing your time. If you don't set goals, then you'll be unable to discern how you can make the most efficient use of your time. The main goal here is to give guidelines for creating realistic goals and examining the various types of goals available. We must also begin changing our thinking to help us believe that our goals are possible and start making the necessary actions to achieve them.

Regarding goal-setting it is possible to apply a rule that is that is known as"the Pareto Principle. It was developed in the late Italian sociologist and economist Vilfredo Federico Pareto. it is believed that 80percent of the outcomes you achieve could be accomplished in a mere 20 percent of our lives. This was a concept he came up with when he realized that 20percent of families living in Italy were able to hold an 80% share of the country's wealth. Regarding working and managing time The Pareto Principle states that 20 percent of your jobs require around 80percent of your time because it is the ones that are important. The remaining 80 percent of tasks that take 20 percent or more of your time, are less crucial to your daily life and ought to be given less importance. This is the reason why you should follow the Pareto Principle can also be known as the 80/20 Rule (Time Management Pareto, ABC & Co., n.d.).

This is a proven method of managing time and prioritizing tasks and identifying issues with scheduling prior to implementing plans for work which is concrete. To apply the Pareto Principle you need to be able to clearly define your goals and differentiate the essential ones from the non-important. Be aware of the strengths as well as weaknesses, so you can determine the successful factors that allow you to attain 80percent of your success with a 20% commitment to time. Below are some illustrations of how to apply the Pareto Principle:

* 20 percent of the customers who are in business are the main reason 80 percent of sales.

* 80percent of jobs at work are completed in 20

percent per hour.

* 80 percent of the most important decisions are made within 20 percent times.

In each of these situations the remaining 20% of the time is allocated 80percent of your time, because they are more important to your achievement.

Planning and Goal-Setting as well as Time Management

Goal setting and managing time are two of the most important aspects to achievement, whether in business or career, or something connected to our personal lives. If you're making goals but aren't setting them, honestly, I'm not sure what you're working towards in your life. Goals help you focus and assist you in determining what aspects of life you should be focused on. If your answer to me is "Well I'm just hoping to wander around and explore the world for the entire time," my response to this is "Don't you want to establish goals that will help you determine what you'd like to do and the most effective ways to achieve it, and innovative strategies to reduce your expenses?" Goal setting can be exciting and fun when you sit down to make plans for your future.

Time management plays a role in the context of the quantifiable aspects of setting goals. Let's examine the business aspects of setting goals. In the beginning setting goals gives direction to everyone who is involved in the business, that includes the CEOs, managers employees, contractors vendors, and customers as well as other vendors, customers, and employees. As you can see, a range of individuals are affected. Setting goals helps everyone be in the same boat so there's no miscommunication.

Everyone who is involved in the company will be better able to manage their time more effectively because they'll know what actions they need for them to complete to achieve the desired end goal.

Every goal you set must have a time frame. It's not enough to simply say that you're going to achieve something only to decide not to set a date. Otherwise, you're making a statement that is random but not creating goals. When there's a deadline it means that you have something to strive for. It is true that deadlines can be modified in the event of need however, at the very the very least, you have a goal in your head. If you're part an organization, whether large or small, all those involved will be aware of the planned timeframe for completing the goal. They are more likely to take the necessary actions. When you are aware that a task will be completed in just five days, you'll be more determined to finish it than the case where there isn't a specific date.

If goals are set within an organization, it's less likely employees are wasting their time working. If there are a defined amount of objectives that are defined that employees are always given an obligation to meet. There are always targets to achieve. This is good for the morale of the employees since the majority of people seek a sense direction when they go to work, and don't wish to be insignificant. Setting clear deadlines and goals at work will never leave employees wondering what they should do next. Naturally, employees should be accountable for their actions, too.

A company who is focused setting goals and action steps to achieve targets, and effective time management strategies will be a stronger competitor in the industry they're in. The company will be able to get things completed, and their customers and clients will appreciate it, too. It's the same for the personal life of a person. If they establish goals that have clear deadlines, then they'll have something tangible to strive for and not be able to think about what they should be doing each day. If they establish an objective and devise strategies to reach it the routines for their day are set.

The most important thing to remember is that goal setting is an essential initial step in managing time. Without it, there'll be no direction , or desired result. If nobody has goals, nothing will get done, not even having time and having fun. The people would wander aimlessly and would have no meaning within their daily lives. Set goals that are concrete and you'll be amazed by how much more focused you are to your time.

Setting Goals in a manner that Does the Job

Set goals is a simple and crucial way to decrease the distance you have to travel from the point you're at to where you would like to be. It's not a secret that those who have goals have much greater success in every aspect than those who do not. This article will be on how to set goals correctly. There are various kinds of goals that are more effective than others when it comes to getting the task accomplished. When you are beginning to build your time management abilities It is essential to be aware of the type of goal you're setting , as there are many different goals that are not created to be equal. There are a few differences when setting goals that could make a difference in your success or not.

Behavior Versus Outcome Goals

A goal for the end result is when you're focused on the outcome. For example realtors may set a goal to sell 10 homes before the at the end of the month or a person who has started an exercise regimen might want to shed five pounds in of the initial week. Like the title suggests it's all about the results. The issue with these kinds of objectives is that they're out of your control in a certain amount. For instance an agent cannot make someone buy a house, and an person who is trying to lose weight may not be aware of how their body is going to react to exercises. There are numerous other factors that could affect the outcome. However, when these elements happen and you don't achieve your goals for the outcome despite all your efforts, it can cause lots of stress and make you feel like you are a success, but that's not the situation.

The solution is to set behavioral goals that separate your actions from external influences. The best thing about these goals is that they're not focused on results and are more focused on what you're doing. For instance rather than saying that you'll lose 5 pounds at the end of the week through exercise then tell yourself that you'll exercise five times during the week. You are able to control the amount of times you exercise and determine what the real outcomes of your exercise will be.

To focus on your goal for behavior consider the result you'd like to see, and decide what you need to do to reach that goal. Referring at the real estate agent: if they are hoping to sell 10 homes before the close of the month then they can establish an objective to contact up to 50 potential clients within that timeframe. It is important to focus on the behavior you are able to influence as your primary objective and not get so focused only on end result. You could definitely set both kinds however, keep the end goals in the forefront of your thoughts while the goal of your behavior is at the top of your list. Consider your actions as your primary goal, and the outcomes as topping to the cake. Whatever way you go, you'll still be able to enjoy cake. This will keep you from getting frustrated when you're done.

Approach vs Goals to Avoidance

A goal to avoid is an attempt to stay clear of any negative outcome, and when someone has lived for long enough, they will realize this isn't possible. The act of avoiding negative outcomes could easily trigger a chain of negative thoughts. It can also strengthen those outcomes you wish to see to avoid. Examples of avoidance goals are:

* Don't lose your job because of that new work.
* Don't risk losing your home.
* Do not upset your family members or friends.
* Don't miss your midterms.

Make sure you don't make a mess of your eating plan.

An approach goal occurs an attempt to reach an outcome that is positive. This type of goal provides you a positive perspective by uplifting your mood. Moving from avoidance to approach goals is as easy as changing the meaning of words. Make your words change a

to alter your thinking. Here are some examples:
* I'm going to do incredible at my new job.
* I'm going to convert my house into a house. My family and friends will always cherish me for who I am.
* I'll pass my midterms.
* I'm going to follow my new diet regimen.
Modifying the way you say your words can drastically alter your mood. Do it today.
Consider the goals for avoidance you've set and modify the words to make them sound more positive.

Abstract Versus Concrete Goals

Abstract goals are ambiguous and don't provide much guidance or even motivation. For instance, it could be, "I want to workout more." What is what does it mean? How much do you plan to exercise and when do you plan to begin? And what are the reasons you'd like to work out? When setting your goal, it is important to be extremely specific. Take this to illustrate: "I want to work out more and am planning to rise an hour earlier each day from tomorrow onwards and run. I'll start with 15 minutes the first day and gradually increase the duration from there. The ultimate goal is running for 1 hour every day. I'll be running at least four times per week." The second goal is more specific and provides more detail regarding what you're looking to achieve. If you observe the behavior, it's behavioral which means you can control it better.

If you'd like to make your goals more concrete, attach them to a visual. It could be the ideal body shape you'd like to have from training, the house you'd like to have one day through hard work, or the place you've always wanted to go to or visit, etc. A visual image can help you visualize yourself reaching your goals. It is also possible to speak your goals in public and share them with a small group of people to ensure that you're more accountable to accomplishing them. People are more likely to accomplish things because they know that people are interested.

As you can see, there's some science behind the process of setting goals. It's not as easy as saying you want what you want, though it is a great first step. If you are setting your goals, they must make it as crystal clear as is possible. You need to know what you are looking for, or else you'll never reach it. It is much more likely to be distracted by unclear goals than with clear goals. Here are a few examples of goals that are clear versus vague ones. Let me start with some unclear ones:

* I'm looking for an opportunity to work in a new place.
* I'm trying to shed weight and feel better.
* I'd like to live more of a social lifestyle.
* I would like to have more positive relationships with my children.

Now, let's look at some goals that are more clearly defined:

* I'll send my application to 5 different businesses this week, and each week thereafter, with the hope to find a new more lucrative job by the close of the month.
* I'll study new meals plans that I can implement into my lifestyle and begin a new workout routine tomorrow, going for a workout at least five times a week. This way I'll be feeling healthier and lose weight.
* I'll commit the Saturday evenings I have to go out with my friends, or myself, at least, once a week, to build a more an active social life.
* I'm looking to build a stronger connection with my children and will take a break each

evening at 6:00 pm and spend the final few hours of each day with my kids. We'll watch movies and eat dinner together or have a night out for a night out with our family.

If you decide to set an objective, ensure that you have a clear idea of what you're hoping to achieve. If not, it's time to evaluate your current situation and determine what your life's goals should take you from here.

Then Breaking Down Your Goals

If you've established a clear objective, it's the time to control it by breaking it into a series of steps. This is essential since most goals can't be accomplished in a single action. It is necessary to take a series of steps to reach the place you want to be. If the gap between where you'd like to go and the place you're at today is too large the focus on this could result in failure. Better to concentrate on techniques, strategies and actions you can implement every day to bring you closer to the ultimate goal.

I have previously discussed how thinking about the bigger view isn't practical when you're working. So dissecting your objectives is the most sensible step to begin taking the right path. If your ambitious goals aren't followed by actions and actions, you'll soon feel disoriented and lose all enthusiasm.

The first step is to set goals. After you've been crystal in your mind about what you would like to achieve then it's time to begin to break it down. Create milestones to help you achieve your objectives. These are little achievements that you'll strive for when reaching your final goal. For instance, if you would like to take part in a 20-mile race but haven't been on bicycle in a while ago, it's not recommended to go for 20 miles right away. Instead, you should create goals similar to the ones below:

* Riding for one mile on the first day.
* Run five miles at the beginning of the week.
* Complete 10 miles before the at the end the second week.
* Complete 20 miles before the beginning of the month.
* Cut down the time it takes to cycle in 20-mile rides by 30 seconds per week.

These are only examples of milestones and you are able to set your own according to your needs. Take your time and go at your own speed but make sure you're moving! Milestones aren't the only way to achieve great things and you are able to celebrate yourself for having achieved them.

After creating an outline of milestones and a milestone map, you can create your task list in order to hit that first step. Concentrate on the initial task, followed by the milestones, then your ultimate objective. For more complex tasks you can reduce them into smaller tasks that will be accomplished in one session. Subtasks can make the task easier. They can be accomplished in the short-term as you'll be able to enjoy an endless stream of rewards. In the end, completing tasks and subtasks can be an enjoyable process also, since you will achieve many achievements.

It is possible to sketch out your whole plan from beginning to end, however if you find it too daunting it may be best to outline the specific goals and milestones first. Like your goals, your tasks and milestones can't be unclear. They should be clearly defined and with precise dates. If you fail to meet one aspect then the entire procedure will be played too.

Chapter 5: Making Attitude Changes

While I've identified the importance of prioritizing however, what I did not point out is that most times our priorities are not aligned. Simply put prioritizing means putting things in neat boxes that give your life an order. However, the issue is that the work box gets larger and larger while the fun and home box shrinks and gets smaller. Over the last couple of years, specifically, the desire to be bigger and more successful has been an instant phenomenon. We all want to make more money, have a larger home and a better vehicle, The list could go on on. However, in this race we end up losing out on living life. In the end, that's the essence of time management about: being able to manage your time and work schedule with your private life , so that you are able to stop and take in the sounds of the birds or the smell of wet mud following a heavy shower.

The measure of success is how big your home and the post you have within your business. This is what media and businesses claim it should look as. Psychologists have observed that people who are happy and can make that the fun box as big as their workbox, are actually filled with joy and energy, and thus are better at their job. They aren't resentful. They don't suffer from this negative attitude which goes hand in hand with having fun and putting work first.

However, it's not something you can make immediately. Through your entire life, you've absorbed the predominant belief that more money equals achievement and success. Time management is a prerequisite for doing more work and that you should be more knowledgeable than your colleagues to stand out. The only thing you require is a shift in attitude to a total one-eighty, which can help you become more efficient and productive, while enjoying every moment that life offers you. This is the number ten: relearning your mindset.

Habit No. 10 - Recognizing Your Own Worthiness

Adults assume the burden of a lot of responsibility for ourselves. One of the primary reasons why children live their lives better than us is that they don't need worries about making bills, or financing an education, or repaying student loans, and on. Adulthood is definitely a time of freedom however, this freedom comes with a sense obligation, particularly when we get married and start raising children of our own.

We begin to prioritize differently. When you're in a relationship and are living on your own and have no one else around, your obligation is lower, because you're only required to look at yourself. It doesn't mean you aren't required to take charge of yourself, just that you've got a less things to be concerned about. The family, while acknowledging the reasons it is an essential aspect of life, comes with it's own set of issues and difficultiesthat are often portrayed by society as well as the press.

In fact, we learn from a young age that selflessness is a good quality. We shouldn't prioritize our own needs over the requirements of other people. We have adopted this notion to the point where it is now detrimental to us. And the worst part is we don't even know that it is happening. Your parents were the ones who taught you this essential idea, they didn't say that you should throw yourself to the ground and let yourself be at the bottom of the pile.

A lot of people believe that selflessness is an attribute that is positive and they apply it to the extent that is detrimental to who they really are. As an example, if give other people the upper hand all the time, you're not bringing yourself happiness. What is truly selfish would be to put yourself in a position that you're higher on the list of priorities than anyone other. To simplify There is only one ice cream in the world and you're with children. Both of you want the Ice cream. You consume it. The child is upset because they didn't understand it. This is selfishness. You have made your child cry. However, it's within the possibility of admitting that you too wanted it and the media would make you believe that you must be a saint and is willing to sacrifice what you want just because you're an adult. It's fine to crave Ice cream, and it's acceptable to eat it. The only thing to remember is that you could have it with the child, so instead of one of you feeling happy and content, you both discover the joys of sharing and relish every one moment that life can offer you.

Being mindful of the body as well as your mind giving some time to activities that are creative or having fun isn't selfishness. As I've said that your time for yourself is vital to let stress go and relax, even if just because you want to reach that higher efficiency mark your boss wants to see you cross. You should give yourself and your wants and needs the same priority as the people around you. Unless you can find a way to become at ease with yourself, you're not going anywhere.

If you're not aware of how important you are to your life, how do you ever be able to give yourself the top the top spot? You are the most important person in your own life. The amount of time you spend in your life defines the person you will be. Therefore, it must include equal portions of time for fun in addition to work hours. It's probably the way your life appears at present, with the sky depicting your job or responsibilities and the small shaded part of the pyramid symbolizing your importance to yourself and to your personal requirements.

Doesn't it suggest that you're that is out of focus? The demands of life tend to take over your life and you're left with no time to spend time just relaxing and being yourself. It is essential to create the form of a pie chart and then in each of the areas the significance of each however it's not enough to just create one and then idealize. You must also sketch out the timetable. In the past you've gotten used to timetables since you're not in college anymore, but they're still relevant to your everyday life. Pie charts and timetables can help you determine which areas you're spending your time and how much importance you're giving yourself in the overall plan of everything. After you have analyzed your data, you'll be able to see how little value you've given yourself. It's when you need to take a take a step back, turn at your tasks and relax.

If you do your work at your home and use the computer, you must decide on the moments when you should put down the computer and take time to relax. It's not about self-indulgence but rather giving yourself the opportunity to reflect on the reasons you love living your life. It's vital to the overall balance that you live. Are you finding that your children are making you unhappy? What can you do to be your best parent when you need to get away? Hire a babysitter and take a break from your little rascals. They should get the best from you. the parent who returns after a few minutes to himself or herself is more peaceful and happier. Kids are sensitive and they are able to take in your negative behavior or anger. Make them smile by making them joyful!

People tend to forget their desires in the name of obligations and, like the chart above, the blue zone eats them up when they allow it. The obligations of life are essential but if you do not give yourself a little time to relax and unwind then you'll be grumpy and negative , and no one would want for you to surround them. Turn off your computer. Take a break from it and allow yourself to be the person you are. It's the most straightforward method available -
Work + home life + fun = A happier you that is more productive.

Here's a great parallel to that. Have you ever witnessed an adult mother holding a child with one hand, guiding an infant away from something that could be dangerous with the other , and then trying to communicate over the phone? It's a common occurrence. In this particular instance the mother isn't paying attention to her children , and definitely not paying complete attention to the phone however she does it out of an obligation. What she's not yet learned is the value of being inaccessible. If you're trying to manage your time it is important to ensure that you are available whenever you require some time to yourself. Many times, we complain that we don't have enough time for friends or family; but did not you consider that the solution could be as simple as turning the phone off to ensure that your dinner time is not interrupted by a work call?

You must figure out a method by which you can receive private calls and not receive business calls while at home. Your employer will be furious for you to spend all day making calls to your family as a result, and you must be worried about calls from work interrupting your personal life. You should have a work cell phone and then turn off and leave an e-mail stating that you will return on Monday. Be clear and instruct your coworkers to contact you only in case of an emergency. If it's something they're able to solve by themselves and they are able to do it, let them without needing to call you for everything.

Be aware that this is as applicable to your family time as it does for work. It is better when your family members know to communicate with you in emergencies only. You can push this further and ask that they should leave yourself while you're relaxing. Many times, we relax and relax only to have children rush in and ask for assist with their homework. Let someone else do it, or just this moment, allow Google to help. You deserve your time for yourself Don't feel ashamed about it. And don't delay it. It will cause you more harm than good.

The most important thing of all is to realize that you're human and you are not able to be able to do everything at the same time. You're limited in your ability to accomplish things because you must relax and unwind, and that's completely normal. It is impossible to be perfect, you are not able to work in a continuous manner and you will never be in a good mood. You are a human with wants and needs and you must meet these to the extent that you are able to put your energy into your job. Sometimes, it's acceptable to take a take a step back to remind yourself you're not a mindless automaton.

Chapter 5 How To Stop Being Angry

There is a limit to the control of what happens to the universe, however at a minimum they control their own destiny regarding how they manage the situations that have occurred to them. It is essential to remain positive even during the worst of situations; getting caught up in negativity only causes you to suffer more. Here are some strategies that you can get over your anxiety and get a handle on your situation.

Think about what you can accomplish

Focus your on the things you can accomplish instead of focusing on things you can't manage. Begin by reviewing your capabilities and engaging in activities that will help you enhance your abilities or which just allow you to enjoy yourself. Then, when you start feeling overwhelmed, you should start doing things you're good at and you'll be able to be able to finish them quicker and feel more relaxed.

Help others.

When things exceed your abilities If you are struggling, focus on making the lives of others better. This can help you concentrate on the positive aspects of things.

Take events that are negative as an opportunity to wake up

Consider negative events as an opportunity to review your the priorities of your life. Sometimes, one traumatic incident can cause people to realize the things they've focused on too much in an area of their lives that they have neglected the most important aspect to them. When a sudden change happens within your own life you're forced to realize that not everything can be controlled.

Don't be scared

Instead of pondering over something, you should learn to appreciate the things that you are learning each day. It's not a good idea to restrict your abilities due to fear of losing control. Be open to adventure and enjoy that you never know what may occur.

Consider it a challenge

Have you ever wondered why people enjoy the thrill of riding on roller coasters? There are many things that provide people with excitement. Feeling out of control and scared can be rewarding when you have overcome the challenges. Consider every obstacle as an adventure and relish the process of getting through them.

Just keep going

Consider how the experience can benefit you. Each time someone experiences something, one grows in wisdom and emotionally more resiliant. If circumstances present themselves that you are unable to perform the tasks you're used to, come up with inventive ways to find an alternative approach. The most successful people earned their fame by getting over circumstances they cannot control over.

Do yourself a favor and pat yourself on the back

Be happy with every achievement, regardless of how insignificant it might seem. You put in a lot of effort and you have to complete daily tasks and conquer obstacles, therefore you should be given an honorable mention. Recognition of your accomplishments is a great way to motivate yourself to push forward.

The most dangerous thing you could do is allow your emotions to pull you down in the midst of an unplanned emergency.

Chapter 6: Tips To Better Manage Our Time Is Time To Control...

We have discussed the importance of time management and how difficult it can be to master, and we now need to think about ways that we can make the most efficient use of our time. Methods to decrease our time by removing the previously mentioned elements can lead us down a different route. I'm hoping to guide you along this route today.

Here are some ways to make the most of our time.
Get into a certain routine
Develop good habits
Do not overstress yourself.
Set priorities and stick to them
Set set goals and stay committed to them.

Let's break them further. They're a bit unclear isn't it?
Get into a certain routine. It is essential to ensure there is a specific routine in place. I'm talking about having a schedule for your

morning, the day at work as well as your night. The routine for morning can be as follows... You wake up, prepare coffee, eat breakfast, go through a half-hour of exercise, feed the pets, and make lunch. Wow, there are an abundance of things to be done in the morning before going to work and you'll be able to see how they all go together. A routine that is consistent will make you feel more relaxed and increase your chances of success over the long haul. If you're following a routine that you follow, you'll have something you can count on each day. This ensures consistency and lets you more effectively organize your day.

Develop good habits. It is crucial to create good habits and adhering to them. For example, ensure you don't take work at home. Are you aware of what I'm talking about? Don't let your anger over work to someone who isn't worthy of it. We're all guilty of it. It's difficult to keep that distance however, it's not impossible. Another great habit is to ensure that you eat all of your meals and complete all the things you need to do. This is similar to the previous tip of developing a routine. Also, do not smoke or drink excessively. It is clear that if you smoke and drinker, this could consume a lot of your time. I know that many smokers are constantly smoking, and it appears that they're always looking for a smoking break. This isn't a good method of managing time.

Do not overstress yourself. This is most likely the most difficult thing to accomplish. Everybody is stressed, and the way they handle it differs. But, it is important to not let stress take over your life and eat up your time. If you're stressed out, you aren't keen on seeing your friends or family members because you're overly anxious over something. For example, perhaps you're worried over work-related issues which is making you not want to talk to your family members or visit them. Your mind is focused focussed on other things. Therefore, you must get your mind off of it, and solve your problems.

Prioritize your tasks and be sure to keep them in mind. It is crucial to be aware of. If you have made an item a priority, you must stick to it. Therefore, make your family your top priority to ensure that you are capable of seeing them, and thus take time to visit them, too. It's a great way to keep your mind stimulated. If you are able to establish that you believe something is of importance and you are able to take time for it. Other priorities include goals like friends, work and so on. Create the list yourself of your priorities and then see what it leads you to.

Set goals and adhere to the goals. This is the same as the previous point about setting goals and ensuring they are kept. Certain goals should be maintained and further enhanced. For example goals that be related to work or the family member, must be kept in mind. It is possible to set an effort to speak with your mom at least once a week evening, or on weekends you can make it a point to visit your acquaintances. When you set these goals, you can take control of your time. You can manage the time you have in a more simple and more efficient manner.

They are all undefined ways that we can manage our time. They provide us with the opportunity to look at our situation by gaining a fresh perspective. In the next section, we will cover the most effective and specific ways to organize our time. These suggestions will be focused on every aspect that we live. We will go over strategies that will help you in your personal time, working hours, and your leisure time.

4. Block social media channels unless they're making money

The average user spends 30 percent of their time using social media. Social media is an edged sword. It's an excellent tool because it lets you communicate with people around the globe who you would have been unable to communicate with in the majority of situations. If you're in the business, it's an excellent tools for business as well. It's really added value to the lives of people. When used correctly, it's an amazing option. If you're not cautious, you could easily waste countless minutes on the internet which could be put to use for other things that are more important. It is crucial to track the time you're spending in social media. It's beneficial when you're working on a task that you are not on social media in any way. However, if you're in a situation where you earn income from social media, it's completely different. In this case, you must ensure that you are focusing focused on business, not the social media. Sometimes I've stayed away completely from social media while working on a large project. I stayed for a long period of time with no social media in any way. If you do this, you'll realize just how big of an interruption social media can be when you don't utilize it in a proper manner.

Stop becoming a dependent on your email and phone
Did you know that there was a time that people did not take calls while performing a task that was important. For example, if dinner was served at the home and it was considered disrespectful to make calls at the time. Before the advent of cell phones were invented, phones were used in every aspect of your life. Nowadays, a lot of live their lives around phones. A lot of people are slaves to their phones. I've witnessed situations when people are in the center of something crucial and they'll put off everything to take a phone call that's not even urgent. They will not even excuse themselves prior to answering. We do not only have standard mobile phones. We have smartphones. We also receive text

messages as well as email and social media access to the internet and more. It is easy to understand how someone could be wasting several hours each day without having their cell phone. have their mobile phone or go to.

Text messaging as well as email
SMS messaging is the latest trend in communication. One of the advantages of text messages is that you can communicate with anyone fast, often in just a few phrases. However, as we talked about in the past, you need to be cautious about the time you spend on the text message in the event that it's not beneficial to your progress during productive times. The same applies to emails. approach, and you don't want to fall into the habit of responding to each email that comes to you. Schedule the time in your schedule and, in the best case scenario, your time off to review all emails. If you're someone who gets lots of emails or texts, it's ideal to reply in the order they are important.

Reducing your time on the television is a good idea. Read more

If you are watching less than five hours of television per day, you will be considered to be less than the average. The average American was spending 4 more than 51 minutes front of the TV screen each day during the past couple of months in a study from the company that makes ratings Nielsen. This is an enormous amount that is especially when that an average person is spending 8 hours in bed for 8 hours of work. If you're reading this book , you probably aren't spending more time than the average person is watching TV. If so, it might be beneficial to reduce some of your time.

There's nothing wrong with entertaining We all like to entertain ourselves. The issue is that you're not keeping prioritizing your needs. It's astonishing the amount of television watched, yet most people don't take a book out and read it book to book once they've graduated from high school or university. I believe it's extremely essential to read every single day. You don't need to read a daily. By reading at least 10 pages in a day, or 15-30 minutes per day can put you in the position of reading between 10 and 12 books in a year. It is certain that you will going to see significant changes in your life by investing this much time reading books. In addition, your time off while driving your car from work to home could be a good the perfect time to read about topics which you'd like to learn more about. I'm a firm believer in and always working to improve myself. You're doing this by reading an article like this.

Chapter 7: Inhibiting Response For Children

Response inhibition is the capacity to regulate impulses and stop yourself from doing the first thought that comes to the mind ("Response inhibition", n.d.). The ability to respond is initially developed by watching adults anticipate issues and prevent them from expressing their thoughts by using words and actions. For instance in the event that a toddler is about to cross a street or crossing point, a parent could warn them be aware of cars , or grab the child's hands and lead them with both eyes on the other side prior to crossing. As children mature they become more independent and they're less dependent on their parents to ensure they are in a safe environment. They can think about their actions before they take them and are also able to think before they act. However, adolescents and children who have difficulty with responding more on external influences and may require more guidance to discern what they are supposed to do and say.

The importance of controlling impulses

Reaction inhibition is important to prevent safety concerns in youngsters and adolescents alike. Children are naturally inclined to play and run around, but they have to be in a position to slow down and remain secure when they need to. Teenagers have to manage their impulses and not follow their own feelings at the time (e.g. drinking alcohol, taking drugs, or engaging in sexual activity) and consider the long-term effects of their choices.

Alongside physical safety In addition to physical safety, adolescents and children have to be well behaved in order to build and maintain friendships. In some cases, children who have executive dysfunctions do not possess an "social filter" that prevents other people from expressing whatever thoughts come to their mind. The children who are successful socially realize that their mouths don't have to express what their brains are thinking! Children who are afflicted by response inhibition issues might just make a rude comment to a friend but not for malice but due to the lack of thought about how the statement might be perceived by other people. Similar to adolescents who have problems with impulsivity may be harmed socially when using social media. For instance, they might quickly post a comment to an individual's Facebook page without considering the wider viewers and how the post will be received. In a flash, a single comment could cause a flurry of follow-up posts and unnecessary drama.

Children and adolescents who are impulsive can also react emotionally to events and could even exhibit aggressive behaviours. They can focus on one aspect of the situation and miss the larger picture. For instance in the event that an individual feels that the other player is unfair or is cheating in the game, he might turn the game around and declare that he's finished playing. Someone with more control of their impulses, on the contrary, might confront his peer by asking whether he's remembered the rules and then asking for explanation of what the other player is doing in the game. Or, the child could also approach parents or teachers to help solve the issue. The child who has issues with impulse control is focused on the injustice and doesn't think about the viewpoint of the other child or what actions are needed to rectify the problem. Finally, impulsivity may be evident in academic settings. Children who have issues with inhibition of response often creates problems when in the class. Little girls might blurt out her answers, converse with her peers rather than doing work, play with objects without permission, reach and play with things which she shouldn't be doing or move out of the seat with no permission as an example. A teenager who is impulsive may speak out during class, and also engage in conversations with classmates. She might also experience feelings of anxiety and appear as if she's required to get up and move about. Both for adolescents and children it can have a negative impact on productivity and accuracy. Certain students be unable to follow the directions carefully and will begin their assignments in a wrong way. They might believe they have the right answer before they are given the directions and end up being off the mark. Many people read the instructions but don't pay to the finer details and end up doing the incorrect thing, for example, subtracting instead of adding, or taking the wrong page.

Children who suffer from impulsivity problems can also be more physically active than children who don't have the same problem. They could be tempted to touch, grab, or even enter into someone's space without thinking about it and may not be aware that they are unsuitable or infuriating until it's too late. One method to stop this is to instill social norms. It is possible to tell people, "Most people like to remain a distance from their peers" or "Ask for permission before taking something they have." Children and adolescents with reaction-inhibition problems may also be impulsive when reading. They might make up their own guesses at words after seeing just the initial letters or read words rapidly but incorrectly. For instance, when they see the phrase "The crown of the king was shining," these kids may interpret it as "The the king's crowded palace was shiny" because they noticed the prefix 'crow' and decided to guess the second part of it. This alters the meaning the sentence and it's no longer relevant. Unintentionally and incorrectly reading could result in difficulties with reading comprehension.

Reading out loud may help teens and children with problems with impulsivity. It may slow their speed and help them recognize when they are making mistakes. Whatever the way that the impulsivity manifests itself in children of any age Learning to put off gratification for a while and control their impulses can improve the quality of their life.

Play the role of the child first, then think later What steps should you do if you've got an teen or child who is struggling with the issue of response inhibition? What can be done to help this skill be developed and improved? There are several methods you can employ to aid children who are impulsive.

Anticipate

Remember that kids who behave impulsively frequently are accompanied by warning signs prior to their are impulsive. They might be brief however, they're present! Your task is to search for the signs, for example, constant anger or overexcitedness, or even agitation. These feelings can trigger uncontrollable behavior, though they might appear different in every child. For instance, some kids display their anger by their facial expressions, while others make fists clench or sound angry or sigh. It is important to identify the signs and to be alert of the warning signals of your child might be.

If you recognize your child's impulse-driven signals, you can immediately redirect them and assist the child escape the circumstance. If, for instance, your child is playing in a game and you can see her getting angry then you could intervene and tell her to take a breath or to stop the game. Alternately, you could remind that she should use words to express the emotions she's experiencing. In the meantime, if your son crying and putting his head on his hands when he's working on work, it might be at the point of running through his math homework in order to finish it. If this is the case it is important to be specific about the reason you're intervening. This can help him learn to recognize the triggers that trigger him.
Sometimes, children don't have the words to express what they feel. If your child isn't able to express what he or she is feeling it is possible to ask "What do you think about at the moment?" to get some clues.

Teach Replacement Behaviors

Instead of yelling or interrupting instead, you should demonstrate how to conduct yourself in into a conversation. The same way teachers ask students to raise their hands and ask children to be quiet You can ignore the behavior you do not want to see or change it to a behavior that you prefer. For instance, you could instruct children to use the phrase "Excuse me" when she is trying to bring something new to the conversation. This can be done by asking her when the interruption (e.g., "Can you please use the word "Excuse for me" before speaking? ?"). It is also possible to teach non-verbal signals, like using the pointer finger in order to be part of the conversation. Model these nonverbal and verbal actions and demonstrate them clearly. For example, you could be able to say "See what I did to speak to my friend even though she was conversing with somebody else? I went over to her and waited for her to stop talking, then I told her, "Excuse me." This is how you can attract attention to someone without being unfriendly." Sometimes something that seems obvious to an adult needs to be explained to children with problems with impulsivity.

It is essential to teach youngsters and children who are impulsive what to do , not what they should not do. This can be accomplished by changing the way you speak. Instead of saying

"Don't disrupt me" you could simply say "Say "Excuse Me" while I'm speaking" as well as "Wait until I'm finished talking, please." This way your child will know what to do next time.

Catch These Guys Being Good

Children with response-inhibition and impulsivity issues are usually stuck in a negative-feedback loop. Most often, they engage with adults when they are being reprimanded (e.g., "Don't talk out loud" or "Wait to be called upon"). ."). This could put stress on the relationship between parents and children since they have less positive interactions. One approach to mitigate this is to check for desirable behaviors in children. If you observe your child is doing something well take note of the act in the form of "good" and then praise them. It is crucial to be precise and sincere. It is possible to say, "I like how you did not interrupt me while I made the phone call." Teens and children are able to read untrue praise with ease.

When children act out in a rash manner and are impulsive, they usually require brief redirection, not lengthy lectures. A couple of sentences will suffice. A statement like "I would like to request permission for the use of my stuff first. Is that possible?" works better than "Why do you keep taking my belongings? I've repeatedly told you! Stop doing this!" Kids tend to ignore you when you choose to use the other speech.

Teach your child to stay clear of Making a few mistakes

Alongside behavioral inattention, there are kids with problems with reaction inhibition who commit blunders when they are working on their academic work. The kids often miss instructions, miss-read information or begin assignments without having a clear idea of what they should do. In addition, they can get caught up in problems only to become lost in the process.

Seek out patterns

The first step to help children who have impulsivity issues is to determine the kinds of school work they struggle with. Are they more likely to make mistakes that are not their fault in reading or math tests? Do they tend to miss words when writing since they're keen to get their thoughts out? Do they find visually "busy" homework assignments a challenge for the child? Do you notice them not paying attention basic math concepts like addition to, subtraction, multiplication and division? Discuss with your child's teacher whether their insanity leads to errors that are not considered to be correct in all subjects , or just one or two. This way, it is easier to identify patterns of difficulties that need to be dealt with.

Teach Sequences

The teaching of routines or procedures to ensure accuracy is one method to assist children who are impulsive. Once you've identified the areas that require your focus, you can create an order that can be applied to similar tasks. For instance, if you find that your child is having difficulty solving words-based math questions because he is prone to skim the questions, you could introduce a sequence to solve word problems:

1. The entire issue is read out loud.

2. Draw a sketch of the issue.

3. Find the key words to give clues to the math equation (e.g. more than than less than, equal to as well as what is the total number).

4. Create the issue.

5. Find the issue.

6. Check your work. Does your answer seem to

be logical?

For another example, when writing, you could teach the basics of proofreading to ensure that your child remembers the steps to take after they have completed a sentence paragraph. One of the most popular is the COPS method.

Capitalization: Ensure that the first word of each sentence is capitalized and that proper adjectives have been capitalized.

Overall: What does the overall design and reading ability in the text? Be sure to check the spacing as well as legibility, indentation, and the spacing of the paragraphs and completeness of the entire thing.

Punctuation is correct? Do the statements contain periods? Are the questions marked with questions marks?

Spelling Do you know the correct spelling?

In general, the sequences should be brief and easy with between three and six steps. You may partner with the teacher of your child to help them master the process, since that they might already be using them in class. Your child can write the steps written on the back of a Post-it note or index card to use for use at home as well as at school, so that they can begin to develop a system for solving multi-step tasks.

Anticipate

An effective way to start in teaching your child how to anticipate the requirements of a project before jumping into it is to ensure that they comprehend the demands. Most children who have trouble with impulsivity do not take the time to take the time to look over what they're expected to accomplish. If your child is given an assignment -- for instance an assignment, for instance ask her to read the instructions aloud before beginning, take a examine the numbers and the type of problem and then repeat what she's understood your in their own language. After the work is completed, look to determine if she's completed all of the tasks. This will help children realize the fact that they might have to consider what they will be required to complete before they begin. In the event that they don't, they could not complete certain parts of the task.

Highlight visual details

Another option for students who become impatient when they are working on their homework is to focus their attention on specific details or important information. Highlighting is one method to accomplish this, but it should be explicitly taught. If you don't, you'll find random things highlighted or too many highlighted. For instance, you could make your child draw the steps of the written assignment using different shades as you go through each step. When you're working on a math-related problem both of you can review each step and assign it a color (e.g. subtraction in pink or yellow for subtraction, etc.). Keep the same colors you use and engage your child in choosing which color corresponds to the particular operation.

Children who struggle with reaction inhibition are especially likely to make mistakes when taking multiple-choice tests. This is due to the fact that there are distracting and purposely confusing items which appear to be correct, but aren't. Learn strategies for your child including reading through all items, even when they believe they've already identified the correct one and then use the elimination method to enhance their multiple-choice exam-taking abilities.

Check your work

A child with impulsivity or reaction-inhibition issues will usually not be able to check their work. They're just glad they have completed their task and want to move onto the next task. It is important to get your child to be in the habit of looking over their assignments. Your child, for example is able to determine if you did the task properly, and whether the answers are clear or not.

The teaching of proofreading skills is a helpful tool for evaluating the quality of their work. It is important to establish an exercise to check your child's work. Make sure not to assume the role of the "checker" however. It is best to involve your child to check the work on their own by guiding them through the procedure instead of taking over the task for them.

Chapter 8: Deadlines For Meetings

The ability to be punctual is an attribute that cannot be overlooked. People who are punctual are more likely to succeed and make the most they can from life. As we've said before time is the most important resource. What you do with your time will determine the level of your success.

This chapter will help you understand the best way to achieve your goals by increasing your performance.

Begin in the early hours
The earlier you begin and finish, the quicker you'll complete, which will allow you to be ahead of the rest.

Eliminate distractions
While you're working, make sure you are tidy for yourself and take away any items (and in fact, anyone) that you don't have the need for. Keep in mind that there is a time for everything, and when it's time to go to work it's just what

you do: you work.

Set earlier deadlines
If you have a deadline of 5 pm and you have a deadline of 5 PM, set the self-imposed deadline of 3pm. Try this out to test yourself and see if it is possible to test your limits. When you succeed you will be rewarded in the right way.

Make sure you are quick and precise.
Be active and enthusiastic But don't be impulsive and reckless. You must strike the right balance between speed and accuracy. Speed is essential since it allows you to do more than precision, but it is also crucial to make sure that you don't need to re-do anything.

Work on your own
There is no need to be able to handle everything on your own every day, however, when the time comes to shove, it's important that you're capable of handling things yourself. Because working with others is inevitable, find those you can count on Don't limit yourself to one person who is there to support you.
Make backup plans

Prepare yourself in case problems occur because they could. Therefore, think quickly and determine various ways to get things completed.

Make a list.
A list does two goals: 1.) it aids in organizing your tasks that you have to complete and also 2) it lets you observe your progress. You can try it out and notice that crossing out the items in your list after you've completed it feels great.

Be extremely, very disciplined
Create an idea and a schedule that you will follow.

Find a suitable setting
You should work in a setting that can help you achieve your goals. Consider the way in which your equipment or supplies are organized, and how your work space is kept from distractions, and whether you've got everything you need available at your fingertips.

As you strive to achieve the goal, it's common to run into physical blocks or periods that you lose focus. The best solution is to include short breaks into your routine which range from five to ten minutes breaks during which you take a walk, drink a beverage or engage in something else to reenergize yourself.

Chapter 9: Time Tools For Management

Do you know the value of you are worth for your work time? If you're in an industry that charges your clients hourly, you'll have a great idea, but for the majority those who work in this field, it is difficult to begin determining the value of their time.

It is essential to be able to assign a value in dollars to your time, as this will allow you concentrate on the tasks that matter most to you and stay clear of jobs that offer minimal or no value to you.

Finding time to do more

If you've never utilized an activity log before, it's the right time to begin, because it will reveal exactly what you are doing with your time, and ways you could be able reduce your workload while becoming more productive, and not needing to work all day long to achieve this.

How do you maintain an Activity Log

In a spreadsheet, add the column headings below:

Date / Time
Description of Activity
What do you feel?
Duration
- Value (none, low. Medium, high)

When you've completed your challenge, don't alter your routine, note down every action you take as you perform it. Each time you start something new like making coffee, answering emails, and so on, note what you did at the duration along with how your feeling.

The activity log is a great resource for learning.

After you've collected a number of days of your work, you can look over the log and you may be amazed at the amount of time you've devoted to things that were not priority. you'll be able to determine the times of the day when you are at your best as well as when you have breaks, and so on.

If you've completed a complete analysis, you can increase your efficiency by using these:

Remove or delegate tasks which aren't really yours to do, such as tasks that someone else within the organization is expected to do. Your most important work tasks should be scheduled to be completed during moments when your levels of energy are at their most high.

Reduce the time spent moving from one task to another, like responding to emails only once or twice daily.

Reduce the time you spend to do things like making drinks, and divide the time between your office staff instead of everyone having in to prepare their own drink.

To Do Lists

Are you overwhelmed by the volume of work you need to complete, or that you are late to deadlines? This and similar reasons are all signs of not following an agenda.

The list should have the most crucial tasks on top, and reduce to the lower tasks that are most important. Making a list of tasks is a must-have tool for fighting off work stress.

When you do it the right way, when you do it correctly, you'll find that you're organized and feel less stressed since you feel confident that you've not left any item. While keeping a well planned out list may sound easy however, it's amazing that so many people are unable to utilize these lists.

Preparing your to-do list

Note down all the tasks you'll need to finish. For larger tasks, break down the task into smaller steps. actions or steps will take less than two hours to finish.

Check your list over and assign priorities starting between A for urgent/super important to F for not important and non-urgent.

Rewrite the list according to order of priority

Using your to-do list

The process of making your list is straightforward you just need to begin working through it, starting by working through the tasks that are A-priority first followed by B, and on.

The items on your list will differ based on your role and the tasks you perform. Many people find it beneficial to spend the final fifteen minutes of their workday making a list of things to do for the day ahead so that when they head to work, they will know the plan of their day planned out.

Software

In this day and age of computers, there are specific programs which can improve you be more productive than traditional paper-based to-do lists. The advantage of using software is that it allows you to utilize the computer as a reminder yourself of events or tasks that are coming up due.

The computer is also linked to your phone and email and can be shared easily with the other team members. Perhaps the greatest benefit of software is that it is able to be easily updated, instead of having to create an entirely new checklist at the close of every day.

Being Organized and Organizing Yourself

While to-do lists are great for those who are just beginning on their career path, they can become a bit complicated and difficult to manage, especially when you are faced with more pressing tasks to be completing every day. When this happens, it is apparent that you might need to consider using the Action Program in place of the to-do list. The action plan is an enhanced version of a to-do list that includes short, medium and long-term goals. The action program helps it easier to focus on the most important things and prevents you from being a waste of time.

Utilizing an Action Program

Begin by making an inventory of everything that needs your attention. List everything that you consider to be unfinished, no matter how urgent, large small, personal or otherwise.

Take a look at each item on your list. Anything is of no use can be eliminated immediately.

Re-examine what you're left on your list and then begin organizing the tasks.

Examine and prioritize by importance.
Make your action plan that is divided into three categories that are clearly defined:

Next action plan - small steps you must do to help move your projects ahead
List of delegated actions - projects or tasks that you've given to other people to complete.

Project Catalogue - this shows every project you're engaged in, as well as the little task that can help you complete your project

In conjunction in conjunction with the Action

Program

There is no doubt that an action plan will be long, however it is not necessary to go through the entire program each day. Most of the time, you'll be only dealing only with the initial page, which includes your next list of actions and delegated actions list. There are some tasks that are either day or time-specific.

The most crucial aspect to the success of your Action programme is to ensure that you update and review it frequently, for example, every week. This will permit you to remove or archive work that is completed, and to move things from your project catalog on the first pages of your project as you move forward You can also add any additional tasks you have at this point.

Chapter 10: How To Manage People In Your Life

Congrats. You're now the boss. This is a major career move however, the truth is that you're now accountable, not just for managing your time, but also that of the people who report to you. However well you are at your job If your team members aren't working you're losing time and manpower.

It's not a surprise that research studies have revealed that the most important factor for employees is satisfaction with their job. They want to feel that their work makes an impact. If they feel undervalued or not appreciated, they're not likely be able to work to their full potential, which means they're just wasting time.

People who are satisfied with their work are likely to remain loyal, which means that there will be less turnover , and less wasted time making substitutes. Employing skilled employees is among the most effective ways to control your time.

The employees who are content who will do more than getting work completed promptly and resolving issues, freeing you to focus on your own work. They're also the least inclined to become negative complainers. As we've discussed the fact that negativity takes time away from the workplace environment.

Office Politics

You, as the manager are required to regulate the political climate at the workplace. This includes not being a victim of "favorites" and inflicting jealousy among your employees. Be attentive to employees who are constantly compelled to provide you with negative information about other employees, such as, "The statement would have been completed on time in the event that Mary wasn't behind in time." The problem here may be more about Mary and more about the person who is blaming her. If you are familiar with people who are trying to denigrate each other, you can easily stop the problem.

There aren't all employees who are the Same

In all likelihood, every team member will possess their own weaknesses and strengths. When it comes to distributing work, assigning an appropriate task to the person who is best suited for it can make a huge difference in time. If you're not sure of the area they are competent in or area of expertise, make it an opportunity to inquire during the job interview or during private sessions. You want your employees to be enthusiastic. People who fully use their abilities perform their work in a faster and more efficient way than those struggling with the task in front of them.

Be aware of the workload

It is essential for people to put in the effort However, it's not a good idea to overload them with work. This is especially true when certain individuals (possibly your most productive employees) get the majority of work . At the same time, the rest can operate more easily.

The tasks should be distributed equally.

If someone is having issues with the job they must be aware that they can seek help and clarification. This will stop them from delaying things and doing things incorrectly at the last minute or inventing excuses to not do the task properly.

Produce a Positive Environment

The office is a work space and should be professional. However, having an environment that is peaceful allows us to be more efficient. Also, it creates an easier environment to facilitate better communication. For example an evening pizza delivery on a Friday for everyone in the conference room will help attendees relax.

It is possible to find someone experiencing problems outside of work (an unwell spouse or child) and make it easier for them by not needing excessive overtime in such an instance. Additionally, it is easier for people to discuss problems, even if with a joke.

Set New Challenges

It is possible for people to get bored of the same routine, and lose interest. This can lead to less accomplished and spending more time. Create new challenges and new opportunities to people to think about. A great way to discover ways to think of new ideas is to utilize the casual Friday lunch gathering. You can ask, "Does anyone have any suggestions on how we can enhance our activities?" You might be amazed by the responses.

Give Your Employees a Reward

Employers who do not receive adequate compensation will not be able to perform to their full potential and will eat up the resources of the company and their time. While it is necessary for a fair and reasonable amount of financial compensation however, there are other ways to ensure that employees are satisfied. Give credit where it is due and you'll see the individual get more productive than they were before. If you're unable to get an incentive, having a half-day off every month is a good method to reward your employees for their outstanding performance. Why should a person be able to do their best without a payoff?

Be aware of how employees spend their Time

Even your most diligent employees may be inadvertently wasting time, without even realizing they're doing it. You should have your employees track their time for a period of two weeks and review their schedule. They could be dedicating too much time and energy to the wrong task.

Don't be afraid to delegate.

If you are required to control every aspect of your life, you're not doing anything productive. Most the time you spend will be spent to observing others or doing tasks that another person might or should be carrying out. This is an extremely bad time management strategy.

If you've got your self with dedicated

employees you should make the most of the talents of them. Many managers think that no one can do a job in the same way as they do. This is not true. If you are able to provide your staff with new issues and guide them correctly, it could free up a significant amount of your time which can be better utilized.

Achieving success in time management is about knowing the right time you need to step back. Begin delegating little tasks. Once you are more comfortable, you can take on more the responsibility. If you've followed the guidelines from this section, it is important be more aware of the strengths of your team. Make use of them and assign new tasks which are within the range of their abilities.

Provide clear instructions and leave them to complete the task. Trust them to complete the task, but periodically make sure to check their performance.

Communicate Your Expectations

We've discussed the importance of entrusting

work to your employees, however, you must explain your needs clearly. "I require a financial report for XYZ Company" is substantially insufficient to make sense and you're going most likely to be being disappointed.

When assigning a task be clear on what you are looking for and when you'd like to have it. Check to see if the person is the capacity to complete the task within the time frame stipulated. Then, request to be notified one day ahead in case there is a problem. This should ensure that you are provided with the necessary information at the time you require it.

Chapter 11: Managing Obstacles

As you begin to create your initial plan, it's important to understand how you typically use your time. It is possible that you're accomplishing a great job making the most of your time, but you may also discover that you're not making the most of them or using up a portion of them. Of the course, whether it is waste of time is dependent on how much enjoyment you get from it.

There was once an untrained man who spent much of his energy and time putting off his early departure to school. He sat in his kitchen, ate his breakfast and searched to find his shoes, fell over his shoe-laces that were not tied and made last-minute search for his assignments. His parents were furious with him for his resolute behavior of leaving the house frequently caused one or the other of them arrive late to work. The siblings were angry over him for making them miss their classes. The boy was miserable , and his family became less and less understanding as the situation was escalating.

In the afternoon, his mom dropped him off at school. He was parked in front of her, and she saw three boys hurrying to follow her son. She stepped out of her vehicle and helped the boy get inside. After a thorough investigation, she discovered that three children had been a bully to her child for several months. The school term progressed into the final weeks, their behavior increased in severity.

When viewed in the context of how depressing he experienced at school and how the dangers of his actions, his delay tactics were logical. His family decided to take him from the school in which the incident was allowed to take place and enroll him in a private institution with a small class size and there was no tolerance for violence and bullying. In time the tactics of delaying and reluctance to leave the house waned. Family members were able to go out of the house in time, his school grades were improved, and he began to be involved at extracurricular events.

The emotional resistance to getting out of the home can result from fear of going somewhere else or from a love for something happening in the home. A middle-aged teacher started working as a freelance writer, which she worked in the evenings and during weekends. The first few months, the work were a small amount of time. However, as time went on, they started to consume the majority of her laundry, housekeeping as well as cooking. She was awake late and trying to wash, dress and be on time to go to school on time. In her third and final year in this upswing she informed the school she was planning to quit, and she began writing full-time. This solved the getting-out-of-the-house problem, but she was still left with the personal activity/gainful work balance problem.

To address this issue she started to analyze the time she was spending doing different tasks. She found among her top time consumers was the frequent trips to the store.

Another time, she was cooking elaborate meals. Because she often ate on her own it was a bit odd particularly since the goal was to shed weight. She discovered that when she cooked simple, vegetable-based meals, she increased her nutritional intake and also cut down on the time she was spending cooking - an added benefit. Also, she noticed that during regular trips to the grocery store she was more likely to purchase "a tiny bit" to help her get through the day until she could return home and cook a dinner. In making fewer grocery store visits, she reduced the amount of sweets, candy bars, cookies and other sweets she purchased and consumed. Not only did it save money, but also eliminated the incentive to eat snacks.

Modern technology has increased the variety of options to lose time. Conversations on the phone and reading emails, as well as browsing Facebook or other online social networks, and even playing video games and watching films can take up huge amount of your time. If they are restricted to idle time and offer participants enjoyment, they're not necessarily harmful, but it's not difficult to be caught up in a distracting task and then realize the fact that an entire hour had gone by and that the chores or work required aren't completed.

And, most of these issues aren't just for idle time, can hinder the stated objectives of participants. Imagine that you've been offered the chance to visit a country with a different language. You've got over a whole year's advance notice of the forthcoming event which is why you are determined to master at least the basic language. But your spare time is always distracted by something else and you end up getting on the plane for your trip with a book of phrases with you and just the most basic notion about how you pronounce terms in the book.

Over-planning can cause scheduling issues. If you're the proprietor of a sole proprietorship and you are able to accept multiple orders at the same time and you are not able to do anything but work if there is no chance of finishing the work within the timeframe. Long hours of work, with no breaks, can cause exhaustion and ultimately the collapse of your company or it could cause health issues. Hypertension and other chronic illnesses are often linked to the long hours at work that have little rest or leisure time. The long hours of work can lead to eating in fast food eateries as well as not getting enough exercise.

It is among the things that are often overlooked by those who are over-scheduled. Over-scheduling can occur as a result of trying to balance family activities, as well as when managing the business. If a parent works for 40 hours cooking meals, cleans the house and has children go to numerous after-school and weekend activities could easily work an 80 to 60-hour working week, if you count household maintenance as well as running a shuttle service as part of their job.

One method to control an uncontrollable schedule is to begin practicing your word "no." Yes I'm not able to take you to three different practice locations this week. It is not my intention to help you with your chores and they're yours to do. Don't expect me to deliver all your work to you. It may initially be harsh, but in time your children will get the fact that you're not always willing to fill the gaps in their schedules , or to help them out when they fail.

Unplanned events can cause scheduling issues. They can be anything from accidents that require medical attention to repair work on your car, home or even network issues when you work on the internet. It is a must to attend birthday parties celebrations at work, office parties or needing a long nap could throw busy schedules into chaos. Unexpected guests - but will be welcomed - can throw the entire plan into an uncontrollable tailspin.

For instance, a freelance writer felt very satisfied about her work schedule before she fell asleep. She had completed the deadlines set for the day, and for the following one she was sure that she could manage to complete her next day's deadline before heading to work part-time.

Unfortunately her home network was not working. While it was possible to connect her laptop and caused the rest of her household without Internet however, she decided to to identify the issue and then replace the defective router. The time-consuming process included three hours to identify the issue, one hour to purchase a new router, and three hours to correctly connect and install to the computer in the house and the other online devices . That's seven hours of productive time gone. Together with the stress and fatigue that resulted in the total loss of a working day. This may not sound to be a lot to an individual with an extremely tight schedule, it translated into numerous late nights and then a crippling migraine headache which led to even additional hours of lost time.

Scheduling your schedule around unplanned times leaves space for unexpected emergencies and opportunities. Also, it allows for relaxation, rest and fun - three aspects which improve the quality of life and overall health.

Solution and identification
to block roads
(that hinder you from not being the most productive you can be)
O LETTING IMPORTANT TASKS Overshadow important ones

AFRAID OF UNDERSTANDING THE REASON
AVOIDING TRACKING your progress
Overlooking the importance of the need to define specific tasks
O OVERESTIMATING the amount you can do
DO NOT GIVE YOURSELF A RELAX
1. Letting URGENT TASKS Overshadow important ones
ROADBLOCK: This roadblock is one we face often and is the most common reason why that we feel we're not making progress to our objectives. We can tell when we've encountered this kind of roadblock when we realize that we're let our lives dictate our actions. Instead of having a plan that can be followed to accomplish these essential tasks, we are keeping our minds occupied with clearing out the fires. It is a common feeling and are constantly reacting, instead of being mindful and deliberate.

Solution: Start your day by making an agenda to complete the most impactful things first. It is important to determine two or three tasks that are important to complete the day prior to when you fall asleep each night, so that you'll be able to start your day off on the right foot early in the morning. Another strategy to adhere to is routines. If you consistently set aside time for things that are ongoing, such as household chores, you'll always be making progress.

2. Uncertain about the reasons

ROADBLOCK: If I don't understand the reason why a particular task is crucial in the plan of everything, it's simple to push it back until tomorrow. This incident happened to me recently. I put off a task for a few weeks and kept moving the task from list to list. I was tired of it being on our list however, i was not motivated enough to finish the task. After a moment of reflection about the reason I kept postponing this project, I realized that it was because i couldn't remember the reason why it was necessary at all. This small project didn't matter much on its own but it was a crucial step towards a larger objective of mine.

Solution: Make sure you understand what is the "why" behind each task. Examine the tasks that have been on your list for too long, and consider what the reason is for them to matter. Try including "because ......" to the end of every item on your to-do list.

3. AFFECTING YOUR PROGRESS TO TRACKING

ROADBLOCK: At the conclusion of our day, we head to bed and wonder what we did. We were busy but what actually did we accomplish? It's easy to believe that we're not making any progress even though we've been busy all day. Solution: Keep track of your progress and then take the time to look back at your accomplishments. One method to accomplish this is to begin every day with a brief listing of your most important things to do of the day.Another method of tracking the progress you've made is to finish every day by writing down the accomplishments you've made in a notebook. Make a bullet-point list of everything you've completed and add them daily to it before you leave for work or before you go to go to bed. This will allow you to think about your day and remind you of the accomplishments you've made. It's a great motivation to keep working hard to add important wins to your bucket list at the at the end of the day!

4. Overlooking the importance of defining Specific TASKS

ROADBLOCK: If we look over our to-do-list and your eyes start to become overwhelmed Your tasks are likely not very specific enough. If we don't design super specific, achievable tasks, we're bound to be overwhelmed and don't know how to begin.It's the biggest problem we face everyday.

Solution: Stop filling your agenda with big projects and focus on completing specific tasks. Divide big projects into smaller tasks and include the words that make each task more action-oriented.

5. OVERESTIMATING how much you can DO
ROADBLOCK: If we end our day by only finishing a small portion of our tasks it could take the wind from your sails. We set out with such great intentions , but couldn't quite complete every single thing! In reality that those expectations are unrealistic.This could be one of the most significant flaws.We tend to be overly optimistic regarding the amount of work we can complete in a single day. We add on too many tasks and finish the day not getting even just half the work completed.

Solution: Realize that you're not an omnipotent being. Be truthful with yourself about the amount you can achieve within one day.One factor that's been helpful to you is to monitor your time spent on projects for several days, to be more aware of the length things take.Another option is to allocate buffer intervals between projects to be prepared for interruptions, travel time as well as transitions etc.And lastly, work hard to keep your list of tasks reduced to some key tasks that you must be completed today. This will help you concentrate your efforts on what's important , instead of becoming lost in the sea of endless tasks. It's also realistic and achievable, you'll finish the day with a sense of accomplishment!

6. Do not give yourself a break.

ROADBLOCK: When we're experiencing a period of overwhelming and our list of tasks is mile-long the first reaction is to get down and go faster and harder. If you've encountered this roadblock, it's likely that you find yourself in a short of time. It's simple to do, but it's not good for your health. If you're working continuously it's not the most productive you can be.

Solution: Prioritize high-quality breaks. Even though it's tempting to think that you're supposed to work and be productive, you'll get more done when you break during your workday and allow you to unwind and recharge.That time off can be rejuvenating and refuels your body, so that you're fully prepared to resume your work more productive and focused. Set a timer for work for you to remind yourself to take a few minutes of breaks for a short stroll along the sidewalk or a stroll to replenish your coffee cup.

Chapter 12: Improvement Of Your Focus In Your Work To Improve Your Productivity

"Concentrate your entire attention on the task at you. The sun's rays will not radiate until they are brought to the point of focus." Alexander Graham Bell. Alexander Graham Bell
Bell is right. Bell is right: To have excellent results and boost your productivity, concentrate on the task that you have to do. Because that can be challenging for the majority of us this chapter will provide great tips to help you achieve it.

Stop Multitasking
To increase your productivity get rid of your routine of multitasking. "But what is the reason it's doing well on my behalf?" If that is your response, take an honest look at your efficiency. It's likely that it's getting sucked out. The reason is the habit of multitasking especially on critical tasks.
Multitasking makes you lose focus on your work, and can distract you from your primary

tasks. This negatively affects the efficiency of your work. To stop your productivity from becoming less effective begin single-tasking. Single tasking is the practice of that you are concentrating on one task at a given time and then shifting to the next one only after having completed the previous one or having reached an appropriate level of success.

If you're at work on your laptop or computer, shut off all tabs and programs that could distract your work. If you're working at home, turn off your television and phone so that you are able to stay clear of the temptation and focus solely on the work that is in front of you. It might be difficult initially, but once you begin to concentrate on the task at hand and become engaged and you'll soon be more involved and be able to resist the temptation to multitask.

If you're writing your book Smile and feel satisfied with the flow of your imagination. This will eventually get you excited about the work and increase your participation in it. If you're giving your team members directions on a new task take note of how closely they pay attention to your instructions and how you can be more involved in the project also.

Concentrate on only one thing and, soon, your concentration and productivity will improve.

Stop Fussing Over Trivial Details
When you are working on a project don't get caught up in the smallest of details. If you attempt to make everything appear perfect, you'll fall into the trap of perfectionism which causes you to put off your work and can distract you. To make sure this doesn't occur, make sure you concentrate on the job as a whole , and refrain from stressing over every little aspect. It's true that you can never be perfectly arranged. The only thing that is perfect is perfection. is a fantasy. Therefore, it is recommended to aim for just enough and be content with the results. When you're prone to focusing about minor details, take a take a look at the end result that you can achieve when you finish a project in time and then consider that as a reason to conquer your perfectionist.

You can try the 80/20 rule
If you are starting a new project Try to follow the rules of the 80/20. This rule, also known as the Pareto Principle invented in the work of

Vilfredo Pareto, suggests the 80 per cent of the results are the result of putting in 20 percent of the effort in the right direction. That means that if you have a clear understanding of those 20 percent ideas or tasks which can produce an astounding 80 percent result and you can accomplish more faster and in less energy. When you are beginning a project begin by identifying the 20 percent of the areas which will yield the greatest outcomes. If you're launching the first product of yours, maybe it is better to concentrate on the quality of your product it will draw more people to your product and company. This method helps you concentrate on the essential aspects of your business and will increase your efficiency.

delegate Tasks and Authority
Let's face it, nobody is an island, and you can't complete everything by yourself. To reduce time so that you can get the work done that you're proficient at and increase your efficiency and focus assign tasks and authority to those who are more adept at certain tasks than you are.
If you are required to collect your children from

school, visit an unfamiliar client or pick up papers from the storage facility and then collect your clothes from dry cleaning, perhaps you can ask your partner to pick your children up from school, and also to help take the documents out of the warehouse. This can take a lot of stress from your back. It allows you to concentrate more on meeting with and convincing the potential client.

To assign tasks to others determine which team members or individuals are able to complete specific tasks efficiently so that you finish your job in time. Certain tasks require skilled hands. If that is the case, you should find someone to do the tasks for you. You can then give them a reward later.

Mixing Similar Chores

Another method to boost your efficiency and focus is to group similar tasks with similar tasks. For example, if, for instance, you are scheduled to speak at the same seminar and also meet with an upcoming business partner and you want to ask to meet him in the same hotel that you're speaking at following your presentation. Combining similar tasks helps you to save time

and accomplish more work in less time.
If you need to go through emails as well as make telephone calls create an hour for these tasks and complete these tasks in one sitting instead of repeatedly taking peeking into your inbox of emails. This will make the process simpler and allows you to focus more on the most important things.

To ensure that you are on the right path and performing well, it's essential to keep track of your progress. The next chapter will discuss the steps to take in this regard.

Chapter 13: Steps To Take To Time Management

While the term "time management" implies that you are managing time, you can't manage time actually. However, you can control your schedule and your own activities to get the most out of the time you have.

In the hectic and fast-paced world that you live it is extremely helpful to are able to manage your time. This will allow you to control your destiny and live your life the way you want that it would be. The best way to achieve time management is to create an agenda and sticking to it.

If you can master the art of managing your time and time, you will be able to live your without any obstacles that hinder you from living itthe way you want to. There are a variety of strategies and methods used to manage time. In this article you will be taught the most important steps to manage time that will benefit you professionally as well as personally. These steps will help you to make use of your time in a responsible and efficient manner.

Through the time management techniques covered in this article You will be acquainted with the tools needed to break out of ineffective patterns. You can control your time and your life. These steps will help you in many ways , including giving you the ability to control your time.

Get rid of the constant shackles of a non-stop lifestyle and hectic life

Keep your energy in check and keep your focus
* Be sure to take care of the essential duties
* Make a priority list

Learn to work with other people
* Rethink your attitude and behavior
* Work with your organization and not let it rule your work.

Utilizing the time management techniques described here, you'll be able self-control your daily routine and exercise control over the areas which yield the greatest outcomes. You will feel like you have complete control of everything for the first time in your life.

Plan

In order to be successful in planning You must approach the management of time in terms of a skill which must be learned thoroughly and learned. It isn't something you can do in a single day. If you can do it, you'll be able to be able to save a lot of time. It has been proven that for every minute you devote to planning, you will save 10 minutes to execute. The steps listed below for planning will help you to lay solid foundations for successful time management.

1. One day, at the moment

The first step is planning your day ahead. It is possible to use the PDA device, an electronic calendar or the traditional day planner. Select a device that is suitable for your needs. Consider for a while about the best way to make the most of your time. Consider ways that you can offer the most useful assistance to your business.

The benefits of planning ahead are numerous among them that you'll be able sleep comfortably. Because you know what needs to be accomplished and have planned it out you'll be aware of being in control and you can relax. In the meantime, you are doing the things on the list while you rest.

2. Set a timer for your day-to-day tasks

Note down the tasks that must be completed based on your reflections you made earlier in the initial step. On the list, you can arrange them in order of importance. The most important ones should be placed on top and the less important ones to be completed last.

3. Block schedule

Split your workday into chunks of time. Start with blocks of hours and work on a block at one time. Once you are used to hour-long blocks, you'll be adept at budgeting your time you have available. The next step is creating time blocks with a duration of 30 minutes.

Enter these time blocks into your calendar. Time management experts use time blocks that last around 15 minutes. If you have a list of tasks that must be accomplished in the 15 minute blocksthat you've put them your daily planner, then you can start working on the most important things first.

4. The time of the day

Pick the portion of the day you'd like to complete a task. Mornings are best for handling the challenging and demanding tasks that are of top importance. The tasks that are less important on your list can be dealt with later during the day, as they do not require the same amount of effort as most important tasks.

If you have the above plan completed, you're ready to tackle your work day.

Recognize your strengths

"Success is the result of knowing that you have done your best to be the best you're capable of becoming" John Wooden

Every person is capable of accomplishing things that others believe are impossible, as long as they believe in the capabilities of them.

Recognizing your strengths and the best way to utilize them to their fullest capacity, will allow you to effectively control your time. How do you make the most of your abilities?

Action extends

Every person will have certain times during the day when it is feasible to concentrate better and accomplish more. When you work outside of the time frame you have set the chances of success are the same amount. This is especially the case in the case of working at your home. There are too many distractions throughout the day, making it hard to focus on the task you are working on. However, if you know the exact action you need to complete throughout every day life, you will assist you in accomplishing your essential tasks efficiently.

Therefore, your efficiency and optimal utilization of your time are dependent on how you determine the time frame of your actions. But If you do not pay attention to the productive times throughout your schedule, your outcomes will not satisfy as much. Also, they'll take longer to complete.

It can apply to normal work schedule. Find out when in your day you are able to put the most concentration. Concentrate on your most important tasks during this period. The most important tasks, like the names indicate, require your full focus. If you can complete important tasks during your most productive hours You will be able to ensure that they're completed efficiently.

The remainder of your time is spent doing the mundane tasks or even to find time to enjoy a moment of relaxation. This way, you'll be able to maintain a balanced work-life balance more effectively in this manner.

The key is finding the key action points during your day. When you note the primary actions and then organize your day accordingly so that you get the best results with minimal effort. Stop putting off your work

The habit of putting off important tasks often is a scourge that affects all people, excluding intelligent and efficient people. Everyone is susceptible to put off tasks at one point or another.

If you're plagued by procrastination, it can cause an enormous problem in reaching your full potential. This could end up destroying your career over time. The best and smartest way to stay away from procrastination as long as you can.

How can I get rid of procrastination?

If you're determined to put an end procrastination, it is necessary to accomplish three things:

Recognize the triggers that lead to procrastination

Note when you start to delay your goals.

Make sure that you are managing your time and achieve results in a more efficient manner

Procrastination can be described as a gap in time between an action and the intended behaviour. The longer the gap in time between the idea of performing a task and the actual execution of that task, the more likely you will be to procrastinate.

Removing the procrastination

Procrastination's effects are so significant that it is important to learn how to handle it efficiently. Here are some helpful strategies that will assist you to reduce procrastination, and manage it effectively.

Recognize when you start to put off your work

The most obvious signs that you're procrastinating are:

*Spending the majority of the day doing non-essential or low-priority tasks which are not on your priority list.

* Reading emails over and over but not doing anything productive like beginning working on them or deciding how to respond to the email. Focusing on other things instead of your top priorities

* Not putting your work on your prioritization list even though you are aware that the tasks are vital

* Accepting non-important tasks others ask you to assist in, and then spending your day doing nothing but mundane routine, boring and irrelevant tasks.

• Waiting to find the ideal moment or the right mood to tackle crucial tasks

Procrastination information you need to know about

When you're thinking about the tasks you've been putting off about, be aware that when you delay a task with no significance it's an indicator of a high level of prioritization.

The delay of completing a job for a brief time because you lack the time or energy or you're tired, isn't necessarily a sign of procrast. So long as you begin working, even if you have a slight delay, the procrastination won't be any obstacle. When you put off an assignment because you don't wish to complete the work, are you doing the work you've been putting off. It isn't an issue that only affects those who are lazy and bored. Even if a person is confident in his capabilities and is highly active and enjoys doing things and completing tasks, procrastination may occur.

Recognize the triggers for procrastination

If you put off completing an activity, it could be due to you or the task at hand. It is important to know what is most important in the context of a particular circumstance. This will enable you choose the best method to eliminate the habit of procrastination.

The job
There are times when you don't like or even dislike the job you do. This could be the primary motive behind avoiding certain work.
You must realize that the majority of jobs include aspects that are dull and unappealing. The best approach to tackle these issues is to complete the boring tasks first. This allows you with the task you enjoy, with a greater focus.

Your contribution The second trigger occurs the moment you're unorganized. An organised mind has the capacity to keep away the temptation. Priority lists that you make will help you stay clear from distractions and stick to your timetable. This is why you should makeprioritizing lists are considered to be an essential element of managing time. You'll know what an assignment is and the time it must be completed. The duration required for the job will be clear and allow you to start when you are ready, and avoid putting off the work. The best remedy to avoid procrastination is a meticulous plan. Organised people are aware of the benefits of breaking down their work into manageable blocks.

The organization you choose to use may not always be helpful in the event that a project seems too overwhelming to handle. You may doubt your ability and resources required to complete the job, putting it off until the very last minute.

The reality is that putting off a crucial job won't eliminate it. There are times when you're worried about succeeding more than not being able to complete the task. As an example, you might believe that finishing a tough task will lead to additional jobs like this. You could be pressured to complete things which are beyond your abilities.

Do your best to avoid the habit of procrastination

Procrastination can be a problem that you can stop by consistently stopping doing it. You can employ a variety of methods to increase the chances of not engaging in the behavior. Here are some suggestions:

Offer an indulgence or reward when you have completed a particularly challenging task. Note your satisfaction at the end of your task, and then you can reward yourself.

* Peer pressure can be effective in preventing procrastination as well. You can ask a colleague or a friend to see if you complete your work in time or not.

Imagine the unpleasant consequences of not finishing the task in time. This is certain to spur you to stop putting off tasks.

* If your lack of organization is driving you to put off work, then get organized.

* Last but not the least, you must focus on a single project at any time. If it's a huge task break it down into smaller , manageable chunks.

When you focus on abstaining from procrastination to the best potential, your odds of managing your time effectively rise exponentially.

Develop the ability to organize

Even though it could seem counterproductive, cutting down on your time spent working is beneficial to increase your productivity and efficiency. The most effective way to meet deadlines that are threatening is to work for fewer hours and directing the time more effectively.

If you cut down on the hours that you work, you'll be required to prioritize the essential tasks, and also manage the limited hours of your time. You'll become proficient in this field, because without it, you won't finish your tasks on time.

Here's an illustration of how to accomplish this: Set a time limit to your working day. This will help you plan your day accordingly, and ensure that you can complete the things that have to be accomplished. Try to complete the task as quickly and efficiently, until you reach your deadline.

If, on the other hand you continue performing the work until they're finished regardless of the amount of time it takes, you'll find that the work is moving slowly. This is due to the fact that you don't have the urgency to finish the task in a hurry. Therefore, you are working long hours and accomplish less work.

Reduced hours can also have many benefits.

* It helps keep you fresh and active.
* You'll be able concentrate on the task more efficiently while completing them in quicker time.

The most important thing to keep in mind to keep in mind is that you should not cut down the number of hours that you are the most active or during the activity period mentioned earlier. This will enable you to do your best effort, but not succumbing to burnout.

Skills in the mind that help with organizing
Many jobs require focus, concentration on a clear and coherent thought and a strong memory. It is essential to be sharp and alert. If you have good organizational skills you'll be competent to

Processing information takes less time

• Translate your thoughts into a clear, articulate message

* Concentrate on the finer aspects with precision

To help you stay organized, keep a diary and note your thoughts, ideas as well as the inspirations and other things you need to keep in mind. This is a productive technique that allows you to produce optimal results using a minimum of resources. A scheduler or calendar is another good example of planning and organizing your thoughts.

Physical Skills

If you are able to maintain your workspace in order and functional It's also an aspect of your organization skills. If you are free of clutter it is possible to locate things quickly and complete your work quickly. However If you're unorganized, you could get lost, lose, or damage things that can cause havoc to your timetable.

The most effective methods to increase your organizing skills are

* Keep track of items you use

Return the item back to the original location they were after you used them.

* Develop a strategic physical plan and solution to increase order, cleanliness and efficiency of your workplace

Filing Office solutions, filing records keeping inventory management for offices the responsibility for equipment, office supplies, as well as management of resources are just a few of the methods to organize your office work.

Learn to Prioritize

If you're eager to reach your goal of managing your time efficiently Prioritization is the best method to achieve it. Here are four easy steps you can follow to achieve it.

Step 1

Take note of what you must do.

What can you do to incorporate changes into your routine?

Create a list of things you do regularly and the way you do these.

Consider all the distractions that you encounter, such as traffic or radio, television, and many other sounds or interruptions through email, phone calls or coworkers. Write down the distracting factors.

Consider the way of work you employ. What is the time you perform the best work? What time of the day are the most productive?

Consider the time that is ideal for simple or difficult tasks, and whether you are comfortable working by yourself or with others.

Step 2

Decide on the goals you want to achieve, as well as how you will achieve them.

Make sure you take some time to relax while you pursue the goals you have set. It will help you feel relaxed.

Once you have decided your goals then the following step will be to arrange your daily routine and your work style

Step3

The process of prioritizing your goals can be easy, provided you know how to break your work into manageable and smaller tasks. This can be used for simple daily tasks like buying food items, or even a long-term financial investments.

Review the plan of action you've selected, as well as the tasks you must finish first. Prioritize these tasks first, and then finish the tasks less crucial later.

Prior to starting your day, create an extensive list of things that require immediate attention. If you focus on insignificant things, you could take up all of your precious time. Therefore, you should prioritize your the tasks so that you complete the most crucial tasks first.

Step 4

Prioritization helps you control your time effectively and complete your tasks in a timely manner. This helps relieve stress at work as well as in your life. Utilizing specific tools for prioritizing helps to improve the efficiency of your work. For instance, you could try pareto Principle or the 80-20 rule. This can help you determine the crucial issues, and identify which will have the greatest impact when solved in time.

Action Priority Matrix is another tool to assess the value of a task as well as the amount of work required to accomplish the task. It helps you determine the nature of tasks that are major fill-ins, quick wins or low-value tasks. Then, you can concentrate on tasks that will give the highest return. Find out which tasks that you must delegate or save for an earlier date.

The tools assist you in learning to prioritize when working in a team which makes it extremely difficult to determine the most important tasks , and assign them to them in a timely manner.

CHAPTER 14: HOW TO BUILD And RETAIN Active Habits

How to change your habits (and the way you live your life)

What is Habits?

Habits are a set of behaviors that take place outside of conscious awareness. A variety of Habits are beneficial, as they allow you manage your time and work on important and routine daily tasks.

Many people are afflicted by irritating habits earlier or later in life and numerous attempt to get rid of them.

How many of your friends start with the New Year loaded with high hopes to break a bad habit and then give up at the year's end? Maybe this occurred to you too!

Have you got a pattern that you would like to get out? Are you a slave to your habit or master? Are you aware that ultimately, your habits will determine your future?

No matter what you be wishing for in your life, you can't just glide into the life you want, you have to take action towards what you want by pursuing your objectives.

Examine your habits that you've built up. Some are useful because they're consistent with your character, whereas some habits are harmful and do not serve your goals.

Ending a habit includes determination! They differ from addictions because they can be controlled by will but addictions are harmful behaviors that are not at the control of the will. Many people adhere to unhealthy practices because they satisfy the need for an intense desire as a reward.

Habits aren't natural, rather , they are influenced and learned by the environment through an action called reinforcement (reward). Take note of the reward you earn from the behavior you want to eliminate. Are you able to give up this habit and begin to implement an improvement?

The year was 2005. late writer David Foster Wallace imparted the alarm-call to a group of students who had graduated from college: "There are two small fish swimming around in the water, and they meet an adult fish in the opposite direction, who is glaring at them and

saying"Morning boys, how's your water?' Two young fish swim along for a while, and at some point, one of them catches the other one and says"What's the matter with the word water?'"
He reminded the students that, in like the fish the lives of us are controlled by the variables we don't observe: our routines and the naive, unplanned decisions we make each day.

They dictate the way we dress in the morning, and how we fall asleep in the evening. They determine the food we eat as well as how we collaborate and whether or not we work out or drink a glass of wine after work.

Every habit has another purpose, and each one provides an individual outcome. Certain habits are fundamental, others are highly unpredictable and rely on triggers that are passionate and offering little-known neurochemical rewards.

However any practice regardless of its multifaceted character, is a flexible. The most dependent drinker could end up as a calm alcoholic. The families with the highest dysfunction have the potential to transform themselves. The dropout from secondary school can become a successful executive.

Changes in habits are not just an issue to be resolved your issues, regardless of the things you've probably realized. Of course, we all as all have our own habits that which we've tried breaking but have failed. And what about the wonderful habits we've attempted to protect and then abandoned?

But, the main obstacle of change in the majority of people isn't a lack of willpower, it's an inability to understand the way that habit works.

In reality, the routines change to some extent similarly.

When an the smoker ceases smoking, or an organization changes its overall behavior to improve its security policies There is a certain general pattern in place.

As part of their vast research into the underlying causes of habit in the 90s, researchers from the Massachusetts Institute of Technology found an easy neurological loop in the middle of each habit.

Every pattern, it is apparent, consist of three components which include a routine, reward and an prompt. The researchers have named it the "habit loop."

In their research, they analyzed the individuals and groups that had successfully changed their resolved, vindictive behavior, they found that they had all followed the same pattern of behavior and had a clear understanding of the pattern of the behavior. They explored various avenues to win prizes to satisfy the desire behaviour of seeking to satisfy and also hid the trigger which triggered the behavior in any way. In the end, the people who had performed habit change created an arrangement that could help them respond in a distinct way at the lead.

No matter if they were tired that drove them to the cafe or lonely leading people to bars, it will encourage them to adopt the new habit, thus keeping them from returning to their previous behavior.

The Identity-Based Habits of the Human How to Stay True to your Ziels

If you're concerned about a behaviour that you're ready to let go (and you don't?) The steps below will show you the how to communicate this structure so that you can show the change you'd like to make.

The first step is to recognize the Routine

If you are prone to negative behaviors. Perhaps it's a pattern similar to that chocolate chip cookie habit I have.

Imagine that your behavior has led to you gain some pounds. In reality, suppose that your habit caused you to achieve exactly 8 pounds and your spouse has made some insensitive remarks.

You've tried to force yourself to stop. You even attempted to create a Post on your computer that reads no more cookies. Whatever the case, each night you try to figure out how to forget about the note. You take a step, go to the cafeteria, buy an item, and as you chat with your colleagues at the counter, enjoy it. It's a good feeling.

In the end, you feel terrible. Tomorrow, you assure yourself, you'll find the courage to stand up. Tomorrow will be different.

Then, on the other hand, the propensity takes hold.

What would you do to alter this behavior especially when the cookies are delicious?

The first step is to identify the routine. For most people to follow a routine, it's the most apparent view point that you must alter.

Imagine your normal like mine is to get up from your desk in the evening, go through the cafeteria to purchase something sweet, and then eat it while having a chat with your colleagues.

The next step is to ask a few less specific questions: What's the reason for this particular routine? Is it hunger? Low glucose or fatigue? Do you need to take to take a break before tackling another project?

Then, just what's the prize? What is it? Is it the cookies themselves? The shift in view? The brief diversion? Socializing with colleagues? Perhaps, you can also experience the surge of energy which comes from the impact of sugar?

To understand this, you'll need play around with the idea.

Step Two: Test the Rewards

The rewards are intense since they fulfill our desires. We're often not aware of the motives behind our actions, but.

It's possible to believe that we want some online shopping but it's really an additional thing we're seeking -- a break from a gruelling task or the chance to gaze off into space for a while.

To determine which needs drive certain behaviors, it is important to look at diverse avenues for winning unique prizes. It may be a few days or weeks or significantly more.

No matter how much it is, you should not think about rolling out a real improvement. You can now think of yourself as a researching for information.

The initial day the moment you decide to give in to a propensity it is necessary to alter the way you conduct yourself, to ensure that you receive a distinct reward.

If you want to indulge in treats, you could take a break from your desk and, as opposed to walking into the cafeteria, you can walk around the square , then return to work without eating any food.

The next day, go to the cafeteria to purchase a donut , or a candy bar. Eat it in your workplace. From then afterward, you should visit the cafeteria, purchase an apple, and then eat it while conversing with your coworkers.

Then, you can try an espresso. In the meantime instead of heading off towards the coffee shop, go into your busy office with your friend and talk for a few minutes before returning on your own desk.

It's a thought. What you do in contrast to buying cookies isn't crucial. The reality is to examine various hypotheses to determine which desires are driving your daily routine. Addicts who are in recovery discover early on that they don't drink to get drunk but because it can help them gain a particular reward: relief from work stress, freedom from worry and social anxiety.

Do you think you're really craving the chocolate chip cookie or is it simply an opportunity to relax? If you're craving the sweet is it because you're hungry? (In this situation it's the Apple should work in the same way too.) Perhaps it is because you require the blast of vitality that the treat offers?

(Assuming this is true that is the case, then the apple or coffee might be sufficient.) Do you think you're just cruising to the cafeteria to have an opportunity to meet people and share a cookie, which is merely a nice idea?

(Assuming that this is the case walking to someone's workspace and chatting for a few minutes could be enough to satisfy the massive.)

If you are testing the various rewards, you can use an ancient trick look for examples:

Following each step, write down on a piece of paper the three main things that sound like bells.

These can be thoughts, emotions thoughts, unrelated thoughts or reflections of your thoughts or just the three first words that pop into your mind.

The reason it's important to note the three points (regardless of the possibility they're not necessary phrases) has two reasons. It draws your focus on what you're thinking or experiencing.

Studies have also shown that recording a few words will help you remember the thoughts you had at the time.

When you are done with the research, when you look over your notes at the end of the investigation at the end of the investigation, it will be much easier to remember what you thought and felt when you received your reward. This will assist you in making sense of what you have learned.

After you've recorded a few phrases, set a warning on your computer or watch that will last for fifteen minutes. If it is gone then ask yourself: Do you feel a strong urge to eat that cake?

The purpose behind this exercise is to determine what reward you're looking for. If it takes you 15 minutes in after eating a donut at the workstation instead of an item at the cash register, and despite everything , you're determined for you to wake up early and head to the cafeteria your desire isn't triggered by a craving for sugar.

If, after a day of gossiping about the workplace of your companion and despite all the arguments, you still need cookies If you're still craving a cookie, then the need for human contact isn't the reason behind your actions. However in the event that, 15 minutes later, after talking with a person you feel it's easy to go back to work, then you've found the ideal reward -- a brief disorientation and socializing which your inclination was designed to achieve. When you explore different options with different rewards, you will be able to determine what you require to be able to do, which is crucial in re-designing your habit.

After you've figured out the pattern and reward Next steps are finding the signal that's the final part of the circle. From there you'll be able to create an arrangement.

Step Three: Identify the cue

Cues trigger our daily routines. They're usually the most difficult part of behavior to identify since there is a lot of information that is threatening our behavior changes.

Do you eat food at an exact time of the morning because you're hungry? Then, again, because the clock is set for 7:30? Or, perhaps because your children are eating?

To detect a signal within all the noise, we could use the same method used by researchers in the field: identify groups of conduct early and look for patterns.

Tests have proven that every routine cue can be classified in five categories: location time emotional state, people, and the immediate preceding actions.

Note down the information for these five items every time an craving strikes. (These are the actual notes I took when trying to understand my snack habit):

Are you where you are? (Sitting in my office)
* What is the time? (3:36 p.m.)
What's your state of mind? (Bored)
• Who is there? (No one)
* What was the first thing that triggered the need? (Answered by email)

I tried this for three days and it was revealed to be certain that the trigger was responsible for my craving for cookies. I was tempted to eat a snack at 3:30 each day.

I had made sense, in step two, it wasn't food that was driving my behavior. What I was searching for was a short distractionsomething that came from teasing a pal.

The habit circle of my life was complete.

Once you've identified the specific habitual pattern, you are able to begin to alter the behaviour. You can create an improved routine by anticipating the cue , and selecting a way to behave that efficiently conveys the benefits you're seeking.

Step Four: Make A Plan

A habit is a choice that we take at some point then, afterward, stop contemplating, but keep doing. It is commonplace to do this repeatedly. Another way of looking at it is that it's a routine that your mind follows automatically. If I am aware of this signal I'll follow this habit to reap the reward.

To change the formula, we have to make conscious decisions again. Additionally, the easiest method of doing this according to research upon review, is to create plans. In the field of psychology, these arrangements are referred to as "implementation plans."

I realized I was able to tell timeapproximately 3:30 in the end of the evening. I was aware of my usual routine to visit the cafeteria, buy cookies, and then talk to acquaintances. In addition, through my own experimentation I realized it wasn't the indulgence I was craving, but rather it was more of a moment of escape and a chance to socialize.

So I came up with a plan at 3:30 every day, continuously I'll walk to my work space with a friend and chat about 10 mins.

It didn't perform as fast. There were times when I was distracted and didn't pay attention to the warning and then fell off the train.

In different circumstances, it seemed like too much effort to locate someone who was willing to talk so it was more difficult to find a snack at the cafeteria where someone to talk to is also easy to locate.

However, when I followed my schedule, I found that I had a restful day and was at a comfortable level. At the end of the day, I was time to be programed:

The moment my alarm rang, I was able to find a partner and finished the day with an unreal satisfaction. After fourteen days, I didn't think about my routine.

I don't have my watch. I lost it at some point or another. At 3:30, often, I am unable to get up and search the newsroom, and look for someone to talk to.

I'll spend 10 minutes chatting about the news, and then return at my workstation. It's happened without even thinking about it. It's now an habit.

Making changes to certain habits may be more challenging. The decision to stop a habit of texting while driving, requires less of you than restraining an addiction to alcohol or cigarettes. Sometimes, the changes are quite long. Sometimes, it takes repeated attempts and failures. Additionally, it's incredibly difficult. However, this framework can be an excellent place to start. Once you understand how habits work it becomes easier to gain the ability to control it. After that you're ready to go.

Chapter 15: Applying Your 5 Year Vision

How to Make Use of Your 5-Year Vision:

It is possible to follow 7 steps to apply your five-year vision to control your life.

Step 1: Recognize the difference in how you go about your day. You can choose between these two.

Recall how you felt on your most memorable day.

Experience the emotions and discover the places you were most happy having your time on an entire day that was a gift by the gods. Record your entire time just like you did in chapter 2. Once more, divide the actions you take into 2 categories. One group is your levels of satisfaction from 1-3, 2-6 and 7-10. The group is grouped according to the way you use your time in both your work and leisure time to gain a complete knowledge of your life.

Then compare your day with the day you want to live and experience the gap in between that is caused by having control over time.

This is the direct result of the time blurred.

The time of your life is the emotional and environmental disconnect you currently experience in your present life as well as your five-year vision.

Step 2: Identify the areas you can change quickly to improve your quality of life immediately.
While you're making the comparisons between your present day and your ideal day it's essential to determine where you can bridge the gap between your ideal and your present life.

An excellent example is if you enjoy watching films or TV, you can start a media company or start an online blog. If you are a music lover make a course about your instrument of choice. If you're passionate about a subject you are passionate about, begin sharing information and then become a tutor.

Whatever you do to fill the gap in your life, it's crucial to immediately take action to your passions. It's common to see your dream day align with your most loved things to do in the present. If you don't have any hyperlinks you can do the same. Eliminate what's not important in your five-year vision. It might sound daunting, but in reality, cutting out the things that aren't part of your vision will leave enough room for you to realize your 5 year goal.

If you're struggling to find time, imagine you're the time comes to get older and think that you're lying on your deathbed. Do you regret living your life the way it is today throughout the remaining years time? Have you ever wished that you would take this moment to live a life you truly loved ? Or would you be satisfied with living out the present day and three months for the remainder in your existence?

Step 3. Reverse engineer your 5-year goal to your present date and divide it up into easy daily actions from start end and monitor your improvement. Document your reverse engineering procedure.

Take a look at the day you imagined. Imagine yourself going into bed and thinking about the steps you took to get there of your daydream, but start your day with the perfect day that you can imagine and then play a film in your head about your journey back to the present day.

The first time you try this, it's going to be daunting, but it's crucial to be able to take Control over Time. If you don't build a bridge from your ideal day to your current day the dreams you have will remain the same. It's a figment of your imagination.

When you're traveling backwards through time from the day you dreamed of Make sure to record every step you made that comes into your mind. Take a look at the main events you completed and the time in which you completed it. This will help you have a clear understanding of the way you plan your schedule for in the coming years as well as the route that will bring you to a lifestyle that you love.

Step 4: Connect your 5-year vision into your current calendar.

This is where you construct your bridge over the vast canyon we call our lives. Without the bridge, you could be stuck for the remainder of your life trying to find your way through the rigors of life and figuring out an escape route from the endless labyrinth.

Learn what's lacking from your life. What are the actions you're not taking. What are you doing to spend your time effectively? Examine the similarities between the two schedules , and consider where you can make use of certain time periods to make your daily life more enjoyable. If you have time with your family members during certain times of the day, incorporate it on your calendar. We think that we are bound by obligations in our lives, but the reality is that we do not. We are bound to our fellow humans and ourselves. life is as valuable as the person can do to make it.

Make a plan of what you can do to get to your 5 year plan. Be aware that the more steps you take to achieve your five-year vision and the greater energy your ship will gain when you sail through the endless opportunities we will face throughout our lives.

The aim is to create set a good plan for your week, and for the following three weeks. As you're doing lots of effort to create the foundation of your house in five years, you'll need to have to put in a more effort to ensure that the foundations are sturdy. Once you've implemented these strategies then your life will become very easy.

However, before you cruise towards your destination You must organize your journey in a way to ensure that everything goes smoothly. Write down an annual schedule which directly influences your future goals and allows you to pay for your bills. Sometimes it is difficult to stick to the perfect order, however a good example is when you need to bring your child to a class or play with your child on the drive, and make use of the time spent practicing in the car to spend time to work on your goals. You can be documenting your journey in your journal, tracking the steps towards achieving your dream or simply enjoying yourself in a way that you enjoy, it happened on your ideal day.

Step 5: Determine the biggest obstacles to implementing your five-year vision.

Every person in their life will encounter obstacles when they attempt to achieve their goals. Every journey isn't perfect and it's crucial to learn how to overcome challenges wherever they occur.

The objective is to put your dream day the places you are able to. There are certain activities that you can cut out of your life, and others that you can't. It's your responsibility to discover how you can manage your goals so you can use them at any time and in any situation that is appropriate.

The best thing about applying your ideal day to life is that it will be a reflection of everything in your life. If you're feeling that there is something missing in your dream, you can add these into your vision and make sure they feel good while you work through your vision.

All you need is a bit of practice, but making a commitment every day to your goals and dreams will result in your achieving them in the future.

Keep in mind that it's simple to stick to your plan when things are going smoothly But the true results of life are when things get tough. It's your responsibility to get through tough times in your life, and remain loyal to your values and the things you cherish.

Step 6: Develop strategies to ensure that you follow through on your five year plan.

In the course of your first month of trying out your new approach to running life, you need to be aware that you'll encounter situations that can directly impact your ideal day.

It is the only method to beat these challenges in taking charge over your own life, is to stay aware of them and be able to recognize them when they keep popping up. If you're not doing anything that will lead to your dream life It's crucial to record it in detail.

Do you have a question?
How did this particular situation come to be?
How often does it happen?
What do you feel about your emotional reaction to the challenge?
What impact will the hurdle hinder you from achieving the goals you set out on yourself in your five year plan?

Additionally, note times you go over and then take a break from other areas of your day.

You can ask yourself:

Are I spending longer than I had planned on this going to result in an ideal day?

What do I give up bring me the highest level of fulfillment, love or pleasure?

Do I have to make more space in my calendar for this particular activity on days are more productive in my schedule? (An excellent example is to set up large window of time every month to ensure you're happy. This will let you reduce the amount of activity during the week.

Keep in mind that the aim is to gradually get rid of the activities, actions and distractions that hinder your day to day activities. If you're always working late, plan a day that you'll spend 5 or 4 hours at work , and you'll get yourself in the right position to enjoy the remainder of your week living your best life. Whatever the task is important to complete it so that you're more likely to enjoy more satisfaction in your life. Make sure to plan more time for work within times that don't compromise your relationships with your loved ones to make your day perfect. For example: Never miss an event, date or dance class with your spouse , or present your children's the recital, game or your favorite time with your family. Pick a different date.

The more adept you become in balancing your day-to-day activities, the greater energy you'll have to sail towards your goal.

Step 7 Step 7: Talking with your friends, yourself and your family members to get your five-year vision.

The process of negotiating your five-year vision is the key to realizing your dream day.

In the absence of removing the emotional obstacles that be encountered in your journey to altering your routine, taking control of your time, and taking control of every aspect of your daily life, you'll find yourself less likely to succeed.

Chapter 16: Physical Side Of Time Management

This Chapter will examine the most obvious and often neglected part that is often overlooked in Time Management: your physical health.
In the beginning of this book we've spoken about the causes of procrastination but haven't included another of the commonly-cited motives offered by people that are lazy. Laziness, however, is a unclear motive. Laziness is a vague term that is used by people who are procrastinating. In most cases there's a reason for why the people who are lazi are. The discussion in the first Chapter may be the cause of procrastination, which is incorrectly called laziness.

Actual Laziness and How to End It
What are your energy levels?
People who are really lazy and are not just doing things to avoid them due to the reasons mentioned in previous chapters often suffer from low energy levels. In other words they lack

enough energy to complete the tasks on their to-do list.

However, increasing your energy levels is simple when you're willing and able to spend in it. In the majority of cases the reason for low energy is due to poor health and bad choices in your lifestyle. It is possible that you are asleep for too long or too little. You could drink too much alcohol, eat a lot or not eat at all. There are many reasons to not have enough motivation to complete your tasks in the daytime.

Enhancing Your Energy
How can you increase your endurance so that you have the stamina to complete everything on your list of things to be done? Here are some helpful tips to follow:
* Make sure that you have at least 8 hours of sleep each day. This is your time for recharge and is not something you could quickly give up or exchange for another thing without justification. If you're aware of the fact that you'll have a an upcoming day full of commitments you should take advantage of your time for recharge rather than sitting in

front of the television. If you're using a portion of your time to work or something that is important and urgent, it's worth it.

• Eat well by eating in the proper amount, the appropriate timing, and with the appropriate food selections. It is likely that you know your breakfast routine is one of the primary food of the day, that your breakfast should consist of a majority of veggies, then protein and you should drink at minimum 8 glasses of water every day.

* Exercise and stretch during the day, especially during the morning. It's beneficial to include this in your routine Rhythm Routine or Recipe so that it will become an habit. The majority of people believe that exercising is mostly to shed weight - however, that's not true for the most part. Exercise boosts the heart rate, ensuring that blood vessels are warmed up and distributed throughout the various parts in the body. When you've done this, you'll see that your organs and muscles wake up, which causes you to feel more energetic and excited to face the next day. You could be surprised by how efficient this method is in comparison to coffee.

6 REPEL THE LAZY BUG

It is essential that you are aware of where the line is drawn between taking a few minutes off to recharge your mind , and complete procrastination. If your favorite days are those that you're working from home and all you are able to feel motivated about is to sit at your "boob tube" for hours on end Do not think that your home-based business will beat any records. If you're not inspired to work, maybe you should think about choosing the business model that best fits your preferences.

If, however, you think of your business and think about your passion for writing articles, creating websites and the marketing of online sites, SEO, or anything else connected work from home you're probably working that's causing problems to you. It is more likely that your lazy bug already bitten you.

If the work you do is still a source of motivation for you, particularly the results you get from your work, you'll be able to create a better plan to be more successful. Don't just allow grass to grow beneath your feet. Get yourself moving and going in your home business.

Manage your time wisely

If you have your own home-based business it's easy to become overwhelmed that you aren't sure how to manage your time. If you don't effectively manage your time using the flexible schedule that you've come to appreciate it is possible that you will discover yourself putting off your work more and more, or getting inactive.

The first step in managing your schedule is to record the regular meetings and appointments that you need to adhere to on a calendar. This will allow you to identify the time you'll have in your schedule. If you don't utilize a day planner or other time management tool, you must invest into one as soon as possible. A simple day planner could be bought for some dollars at your local retailer.

Make sure you leave plenty of some time for yourself in your schedule. If you don't have any after you've planned all of your tasks, check it over to determine where you could cut time off certain tasks. For instance, perhaps you set aside an hour for picking your daughter from school but you are able to complete the task in 30 minutes. There you'll have a half-hour of spare time.

Be sure that all members of your family have their schedules and personal lives and allows you to plan time for things together as a family. It's easy to get caught up managing your own business, however, it is crucial that you plan time with your family members and not let anything hinder you from attending those important occasions.

Keep your day planner with you wherever you go, so that you'll be able to record the new dates after they're made. Last minute scheduling can get you in big trouble. Keep your planner handy can help you stay on track and allows you to plan to deal with any issues that may occur.

LAZINESS OR FEARS

The first thing to determine the first thing you need to determine if you are looking for the solution to lazyness is where the problem is. It is essential to determine the reason for your lack of motivation. Like everything else, it is impossible to come up with a solution until you've identified the root of the issue. We often think that lazy people must take action However, there are occasions where a more serious issue is present.

A lot of times, lazyness is a result of fear and insecurity. Think about the amount of people you have spoken to in your daily life who complain about their jobs and yet do not do anything to make their lives better. It is because they are scared. They fear being judged, fearful of being viewed as inferior and afraid of failure and afraid of what other people might think and the list just keeps running.

In the end there is no one who is content with procrastination and laziness. We all know the incredible sensation we experience when we accomplish something, whether it's closing a major deal, establishing a new branch, or just launching the process of creating a brand online presence for your home business. Willpower alone is not enough to be the cure for a bite of that lazy virus. Only way to get rid of the habit of being lazy, is to recognize the anxieties that are holding you back, and then learn to overcome the fears. In certain situations professional assistance may be needed.

Overcoming Laszine

Laziness, procrastination, and procrastination are not the best combination. Inspiration, passion, motivation and determination are words you'd like to see associated in your venture. Here are some tips to overcome your insanity and return to get more accomplished at home in your business:

The first thing to determine the issue that is hindering you and preventing you from achieving your goals. Most of the time it isn't so big as you imagine and getting over it is straightforward. Whatever the issue is, you must find an approach to overcome it.

Decide if the issue is something you're able to put off, seek help or simply leave. Most of the time the owner of the business is just too much of an perfectionist.

Make a decision to start the task to be completed, and then choose how you will finish the task.

* Break large tasks into smaller tasks, and concentrate only one small part at one time.

You should tell yourself that you're going to complete the task and that you are determined to complete it right now. It's even beneficial to speak it out loud at times.

Take a moment to be happy with yourself after having completed every little task, and push yourself to do more.

• Set goals for the long term which will provide you with something to anticipate and will serve as a motivation to continue.

Make use of common wisdom in order to keep that lazy bug from your ears. If you're aware of work to be done, take action. Do not delay until the very last minute.

If you manage your business from the comfort of your home, set your alarm and rise from your bed just like you are heading to work. Get a shower, dress, changed and don your clothes. It's easier to be lazy when you're in your pajamas all day. Make sure to clean the bed once you're done and it won't look as inviting when you need to go through it later during the morning. There are many methods you can employ to ward off the lazy bug. Discover what works best for you and stick with it.

Chapter 17: What To Do To Prevent Overextending Yourself

It's okay to say no

Sometimes, we are overextended and we don't realize that we've overextended ourselves. You accept things because you think that you're in plenty of time. You also do not want to let anyone down who are dependent on you. It's okay to not say yes. You aren't able to do everything all at once, so don't force yourself to be everywhere at once. It's not healthy for your mental or physical well-being to be stressed and overworked all the all the time. A lot of times, people ask you to help with things for them, because they aren't sure they want to do it and they are sure you'll be able to say yes. However, a lot of issues that make you feel stressed or make you feel stretched too thin are things you can address.

An excellent example is:

If a friend of yours is on vacation and they ask you to stop by their home to feed their pet and water plants. You're eager to help and feel you are obliged to do so because they have been a great help to you before or are a truly good friend. But , the way to accomplish it means that you must be available each day and evening. It is obvious that if you're required to go there each day, you will not arrive in time or have the opportunity to take a break for breakfast. Also, you'll have to leave in the evening , which means that you aren't able to exercise. It is obvious to say no however you are unable to accomplish this. We've all been in similar situations before. It could appear that you're failing them when you refuse to do so however, your own needs need priority. If you think the situation could put you in a position where you aren't able to complete your routine and activities, then it shouldn't be undertaken.

If you are having trouble telling people that they are not Here are some great methods to assist:

* Inform them that you'll need some time to think about it and look over your schedule. Let them know that you'll be back in touch with

them regarding it when you're in the mood.

Let them know honestly that you are juggling already made too many commitments. If you're sincere, the majority of people can understand.

* Encourage them to find another person who can better aid them in their situation.

When you are able to say that you must make time to yourself first. If you're stressed out by being overwhelmed and stretched to the limit it will be difficult to complete your tasks accomplished. Stress can be a major factor and will eventually have negative effects on your well-being. It's important to put your requirements first. If you're healthy and not overly stressed, you'll be more likely to accomplish more accomplished.

When you have thought about your future and made lists, you'll be able to better understand the things you must complete. If someone asks you to complete things for them, make sure you take a look at the things you need to accomplish before deciding. Your priorities are paramount and the other party must be aware of this. If they understand that you'll only take action in the event that it fits within your schedule, they'll be more attentive to your requirements as well. People don't always consider what you've got happening until you mention it. So don't feel guilty if you telling them you're unable to do something, and then tell the reason.

Make sure you don't overbook your calendar by keeping a schedule. It could be on either paper or electronic (on your computer or phone) but be sure you're making use of it.

Be aware that certain tasks will take longer than others. Always seek out an estimation of how long something will take. This will help you to figure out if you have enough time to complete everything that is on your list. If you are aware that you will not have the enough time to finish your task and you aren't sure, inform someone. Let them know that you are unable to accomplish it and then give them an explanation. Don't be embarrassed about it.

Your wellbeing and time are equally important and if someone cares, they'll be able to understand. If you can't reschedule your job, then request that they choose a different person to do the job. It might take a while but once you get knack of it and it will become more simple. Take your time and allow it to take care of you.

Chapter 18: Importance To Self-Care For Time Management

"Lighten up on yourself. There is no perfect person. Accept your humanity." Deborah Day
The management of time and energy are inextricably linked to each and are closely linked to each. You might have planned an extremely productive day and your agenda will reflect your plans as well. But the fact is that your physical energy doesn't cooperate with yours, then time management will not be of any value. Thus, self-care is crucial to ensure that you are managing your time effectively. Let's take a look at some of the most crucial aspects of self-care. Three pillars are essential to health: sleep, nutrition and exercising.

Good Nutrition

A healthy diet is the basis of energy levels that last for a long time which can help to increase productivity and efficiency. Here are some great reasons doctors recommend healthy eating habits:

A healthy diet enhances mental and physical well-being A poor-quality diet lacking nutritional balance will result in diminished mental and physical wellbeing. In contrast eating nutrient-rich nutritious food your body and mind are awake and active. Research has shown that those who eat fruits and vegetables are more likely to have fewer or no mental health problems. A balanced diet that includes complex carbohydrates as well as proteins, essential fats and minerals and vitamins keep your body active, alert and ready to tackle the tasks on your list of things to do.

Healthy eating can help you control your weight in a healthy way. If your weighs at a healthy level it makes you feel confident about yourself , and this motivates you to be successful in your life. A poor body image can impact productivity and effectiveness.

A healthy diet keeps you energized Food is the thing that gives your body the necessary energy. If this energy is derived from healthy food sources you are extremely lively. However processed foods are known to decrease your energy levels and leave you tired and unmotivated.

A healthy diet can boost your mood. foods that are low in complex carbohydrates can cause the feeling of stress and tension. The high levels of complex carbohydrate-rich foods boost the positive vibe of your mood. In the same way, foods that are rich in good fats and proteins can improve moods. If you are happy and content, you're able to do more work and be more productively than if you're sad or depressed. Healthy food choices can improve concentration and focus - Food choices affect the functioning of our brain. If our body is deficient in glucose, we are more likely to lose our focus and fall to distractions quickly. Additionally, food items that contain high levels of fats and cholesterol can affect the cognitive abilities of our brains, which can reduce concentration.

So, the most important aspect of self-care is making sure you eat healthy, balanced meals on a regular basis.

Sleep

A restful night's sleep is essential to increase efficiency and productivity. It is vital to maintain well-being. Here are some great reasons to sleep. Each of these factors is directly or indirectly linked to time management and productivity.

A lack of sleep can impact your body weight. If you're not getting enough sleep, the odds of gaining weight are high. A poor body image is directly tied to unhappiness and inefficiency. People who sleep well are likely to eat fewer calories - overeating is another reason for weight growth. Studies have proven that those who sleep well consume less calories, which has directly impacting the body's weight. Therefore, get enough sleep and eat well and make the most of your time.

A restful night's sleep can improve focus and concentration - Now you know the importance of concentration and focus in managing your time. If you manage to keep these components at a high level with good sleep, wouldn't it be simpler to try other strategies? Sleep well and awake feeling refreshed and rejuvenated, eager to tackle the challenges that lie ahead of you in the next day.

Sleep is linked to glucose metabolism. Research has confirmed that sleep is linked to the metabolism of glucose. The primary fuel source is glucose for our body, and if your metabolism for this crucial fuel is impaired, it may affect the energy levels. Additionally, a compromised glucose metabolism has been proven to increase the risk of multiple illnesses, including diabetes. Health issues and illnesses can impact productivity and efficiency, both directly as well as indirectly.

Sleep is linked to the social interactions emotional states, moods and moods Your personal experience will prove the truth behind this assertion. Consider your morning if you've had a sluggish or nonexistent sleep over the past night! It's not possible to be happy and cheerful. It is difficult to speak to anyone. You're exhausted emotionally even your mood has been depressed. How do you even think of doing anything and let alone at a high level, in this condition?

Exercise

Regular physical activity is an important component of good health that is, in turn, the basis of efficiency and productivity. Here are some good reasons to begin the routine of working out regularly.

Exercise can improve moods. Exercise is believed to boost your moods as well as reduce anxiety depression, stress, and anxiety. It's been known to increase the sensitivity of depression-related hormones including serotonin and norepinephrine.

In addition, when you engage in physical exercise your body releases endorphins, or 'happy hormones that are also commonly known. The endorphins stimulate positive emotions and reduce the feeling of the sensation of pain. If you are feeling sad or depressed, simply stroll around in the park and you'll notice that the sadness is gone or decreased significantly. All of these factors aid in boosting productivity and effectiveness.

Exercise boosts energy levels Incredibly, the moment you engage in exercise (which produces higher levels of energy than when not working out) your energy levels actually get raised. You've probably observed this after just an hour of brisk, short after lunch. It's not like you return from your walk exhausted. You feel energized, and your focus is higher than before you started your walk.

So, if you're struggling to get your energy back you can simply take a quick stroll around the area or in the nearby park in the vicinity of your office. You'll feel rejuvenated and refreshed.

Exercise boosts memory and health of the brain

A healthy brain and better memory are crucial elements that allow you perform better and faster. When you exercise your heart rate rises which provides more oxygen and blood for your brain. Exercise also stimulates the production of hormones and chemical substances that aid in the development of brain cells.

Exercise can help you rest and sleep better. A calm, relaxed mind will help you to work more efficiently when you're stressed and stressed. Learn to be able to distinguish yourself from your emotions - If you can get away from the overwhelmed emotional state, you'll be able to see things from a positive view, and find our groove. An objective perspective of our emotions can help us recognize that we are not just the sum of our feelings and thoughts. We are more than that. This allows us to think through and come up with effective solutions to our issues instead of getting overcome by their problems.

Accept and accept your feelings Human beings are able to experience an array of emotions, including sadness, happiness and many more. They can be good or negative feelings. While it's easy to accept positive feelings, a lot of us feel uncomfortable to accept negative emotions. There is no reason to be ashamed of. Every human being is affected by negative emotions. If you are able to embrace these feelings instead of sweeping them off You will be easy to determine the root of these emotions. This information will assist you to discover solutions to your problems which will result in better mental and emotional well-being.

Reframe your views Sometimes, the negative events overwhelm us to the point that we're unable to think rationally. It is possible to regain the control over your feelings by altering your perception of a specific circumstance. If, for instance, you are anxious about social situations, then consider eating dinner with friends as a means of enjoying tasty food.

* People with excellent emotional health Believe and believe that there needs to be a healthy equilibrium between rest, work and relaxation.

* Feel satisfied with yourself and not influenced by self-esteem issues.

Believe that their lives have to serve a purpose.

* Can be flexible and adaptable to adapt.

* Have fun and take time to laugh and enjoy

yourself.
* Feel less anxious and stress related issues.
* Have developed relationships with others.
If you're physically, mentally, and emotionally healthy, you'll perform at the highest levels nearly all the time. So, it is logical to strive to improve your mental, emotional and physical well-being.

www.ingramcontent.com/pod-product-compliance
Lightning Source LLC
Chambersburg PA
CBHW071839080526
44589CB00012B/1053